Bill 'Swampy' Marsh is an award-winning writer/performer of stories, songs and plays. He spent most of his youth in rural south-western New South Wales. Bill was forced to give up any idea he had of a 'career' as a cricketer when a stint at agricultural college was curtailed due to illness, and so began his hobby of writing. After backpacking through three continents and working in the wine industry, his writing hobby blossomed into a career.

His first collection of short stories, *Beckom (Pop. 64)* was published in 1988; his second, *Old Yanconian Daze*, in 1995; and his third, *Looking for Dad*, in 1998. During 1999 Bill released *Australia*, a CD of his songs and stories. That was followed in 2002 by *A Drover's Wife* and *Glory, Glory: A Tribute to the Royal Flying Doctor Service* in 2008 and *Open Roads: The Songs and Stories of Bill Swampy Marsh* in 2017. He has written soundtrack songs and music for the television documentaries *The Last Mail from Birdsville: The Story of Tom Kruse*, *Source to Sea: The Story of the Murray Riverboats* and the German travel documentaries *Traumzeit auf dem Stuart Highway*, *Clinic Flights (Tilpa & Marble Bar)*, *Traumzeit in dem Kimberleys* and *Einsatz von Port Hedland nach Marble Bar*.

Bill has won and judged many nationwide short story and song-writing competitions and short film awards as well as running writing workshops throughout Australia. He has performed his songs and stories in outback places such as Mount Dare (pop. ten), down the Birdsville Track as part of the Great Australian

Cattle Drive, on The Ghan as part of Great Southern Rail's Anzac Tribute Journey and at the Transport Hall of Fame gala dinner in Alice Springs as a support act to Slim Dusty.

More Great Australian Outback Yarns is part of Bill's very successful series of 'Great Australian' stories including: *Great Australian Ambos Stories* (2022), *Great Australian Outback Yarns Volume I* and *Great Australian Volunteer Firies Stories* (2021), *Great Australian Outback Trucking Stories* (2019), *Great Australian Bush Funeral Stories* (2018), *Great Australian Outback Nurses Stories* (2017), *Great Australian Outback Teaching Stories* (2016), *Great Australian Outback Police Stories* (2015), *Amazing Grace: Stories of Faith and Friendship from Outback Australia* (2014) and later published as *Great Australian Bush Priests Stories, The Complete Book of Australian Flying Doctor Stories* and *Great Australian Outback School Stories* (2013), *Great Australian CWA Stories* (2011), *New Great Australian Flying Doctor Stories* and *The ABC Book of Great Aussie Stories for Young People* (2010), *Great Australian Stories: Outback Towns and Pubs* (2009), *More Great Australian Flying Doctor Stories* (2007), *Great Australian Railway Stories* (2005), *Great Australian Droving Stories* (2003), *Great Australian Shearing Stories* (2001) and *Great Australian Flying Doctor Stories* (1999). Bill's biography *Goldie: Adventures in a Vanishing Australia* was published in 2008 and his semi-autobiographical collection *Swampy: Tall Tales and True from Boyhood and Beyond* was published in 2012.

More information about the author can be found at
www.billswampymarsh.com
Facebook – Bill 'Swampy' Marsh

MORE GREAT AUSTRALIAN OUTBACK YARNS

BILL 'SWAMPY' MARSH

ABC
BOOKS

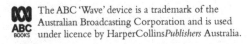 The ABC 'Wave' device is a trademark of the
Australian Broadcasting Corporation and is used
under licence by HarperCollins*Publishers* Australia.

HarperCollins*Publishers*
Australia • Brazil • Canada • France • Germany • Holland • India
Italy • Japan • Mexico • New Zealand • Poland • Spain • Sweden
Switzerland • United Kingdom • United States of America

HarperCollins acknowledges the Traditional Custodians
of the land upon which we live and work, and pays respect
to Elders past and present.

First published in Australia in 2022
by HarperCollins*Publishers* Australia Pty Limited
Gadigal Country
Level 13, 201 Elizabeth Street, Sydney NSW 2000
ABN 36 009 913 517
harpercollins.com.au

This is a combined volume of stories drawn from fourteen of Bill Marsh's previous books:
Great Australian Flying Doctor Stories (1999), *Great Australian Shearing Stories* (2001), *Great Australian Railway Stories* (2005), *More Great Australian Flying Doctor Stories* (2007), *Great Australian Stories: Outback Towns and Pubs* (2009), *New Great Australian Flying Doctor Stories* (2010), *Swampy: Tall Tales and True from Boyhood and Beyond* (2012), *Great Australian Outback School Stories* (2013), *Great Australian Outback Police Stories* (2015), *Great Australian Outback Teaching Stories* (2016), *Great Australian Bush Funeral Stories* (2018), *Great Australian Bush Priests Stories* (2018), *Great Australian Trucking Stories* (2019), *Great Australian Ambos Stories* (2022).

Copyright © Bill Marsh 1999, 2001, 2005, 2007, 2009, 2010, 2012, 2013, 2015, 2016, 2018, 2019, 2022

A catalogue record for this book is available from the National Library of Australia

ISBN 978 0 7333 4298 1 (paperback)
ISBN 978 1 4607 1605 2 (ebook)

Cover design by HarperCollins Design Studio
Cover image by Andrew Tauber/Newspix
Author photograph by Chris Carter
Typeset in ITC Bookman by Kirby Jones
Printed and bound in Australia by McPherson's Printing Group

Dedicated to Keith Carpenter — A Champion

Contents

Sandfire

(Great Australian Ambos Stories)

I grew up at the bottom end of the Canning Stock Route, at Wiluna, Western Australia. Dad was the station manager out at a place called Carnegie. There was no School of the Air so I did correspondence that came out by mail from Perth. It was a great life. I loved it. But when I was nine, I got incarcerated in a boarding school in Perth. They were the worst days of my life. There I was, a little bushie, who'd hardly seen any other children apart from my sister and the black kids and, all of a sudden, I was thrown in with three hundred mostly city types. And I didn't fit. Not one little bit. So just before my thirteenth birthday, I told my parents I wasn't going back. End of story. So I quit school and got a job in the Perth saleyards, yarding up.

A couple of years later the old man got a job managing Myroodah Station, in the Kimberley, out from Derby, so we all went up there. Myroodah was all sheep. But it wasn't sheep country so we went over to cattle. Anyhow, I worked my way up to head stockman on Myroodah, then I got a head stockman's job, out of Broome, on Roebuck Plains. That was great till the multinationals bought the place and all us workers became just a number in their system. So I got out of there and I worked on a couple of other stations till I got diagnosed with cancer in the spine. I don't know why it happened; it just did.

That's when I decided there's gotta be life after stations. So, when a mate who owned Sandfire Roadhouse offered me a job, I took it. And I've been here ever since. Sandfire's on the Great Northern Highway between Port Hedland and Broome. I started out doing maintenance around the roadhouse and I also took on the tow-truck job, going out to vehicle accidents. The thing was, more often than not, I'd end up carting injured people back to Sandfire and putting them on the flying doctor plane. Then, when I went to an accident where a good mate's brother got killed, I thought, Nah, this's not good enough. I need an ambulance.

So I pestered St John and, when they saw that their vehicles were forever doing three hundred-kilometre trips up and down the Great Northern Highway to retrieve patients, they went with my idea. When I got the ambulance, I gave up the tow truck. I couldn't do both. It's up the back now. And anyhow, these days, there's liability concerns and we can only go twenty kilometres to tow someone back into Sandfire, and then we have to call up either Port Hedland or Broome and get their tow trucks to come out.

But it's not only vehicle accidents that I get called out to. Cardiac arrests and strokes are also quite common, especially with the grey nomads. My thinking is: all their lives Hubby's gone off to work and the missus has stayed at home, looking after the house and kids. So they've never really spent 24/7 in each other's company. Then, after he retires and they go travelling, they get on each other's goat and they start arguing. And one of them ends up having a stroke or a cardiac arrest. See, what they need to do is, when they retire they should stay at home for six months and learn to live with each other. After that, yes, then go for a few short trips in the caravan. Slowly get used to travelling together because, later on, they've gotta live in that little confined space 24/7, and that can be tough. I'll give you an example: a couple once came into Sandfire Roadhouse for a cup of tea and the wife turned around to the husband and said, 'Do you have sugar or not?' and I'm thinking, Well, there you go. That's my point.

And before they go travelling they should go to their GP and get repeat scripts and a reminder pill box so they'll religiously take their medication. But no, they'll forget for a few days. Then, to make it up, they'll take all their medications in one big hit. And if it's for blood pressure, it's really going to whack them. Then a lot of them, if they're going, say, from Port Hedland to Darwin and they feel crook along the way, because Broome's not on their itinerary, they don't turn off the highway and go into the hospital there. See, they're always on a mission. You know, 'We've gotta be in Darwin at a certain date and time.' So they'll press on and they'll end up in a place like Sandfire. And then they're my problem. I mean, that's no way to have a holiday. One of my cousins and his wife do a lot of travelling and they take it nice and easy. No rush. They just pull up when they feel it's time to pull up. It might only be under a shady tree. But they don't care. And they hardly ever argue and they've never had an accident.

But before mobile coverage, everything was pretty much word of mouth. Someone would see an accident and then they'd hot-foot it down to Sandfire and let me know. The thing was, they were usually in such a panic that it was difficult to get the correct information out of them. For us locals, with Broome being north of Sandfire, Broome's 'up the highway', and with Hedland being south, Hedland's 'down the highway'. But they'll turn up in such a stew that they'll swear black and blue that the accident was either 'down toward Broome' or 'up toward Hedland'.

What also added to the confusion was when people didn't check the distance. So, when you'd ask them where they saw the accident, they'd say, 'Oh, just up the road a bit,' and you'd end up driving for a hundred k's before you got there. I mean, there are focal markers every ten kilometres, telling you how far it is to wherever. But they're in such a state that they never think to look at them. A while back, there was an accident up the road and a bloke got into such a panic that he rolled his car bringing the message down to Sandfire. So then I ended up having to deal with two rollovers. Other times they don't stop and check what's happened. There was an accident one night, just outside the roadhouse. A woman came running over and started bashing on my door. 'There's been a rollover! There's bodies everywhere!'

I said, 'God, here we go.'

When I went to see what'd happened, two drunks had ploughed into seven cows. The drunks were okay, but then I had to spend the rest of the night dragging dead cows off the road.

So you never know what you're going to end up with. Like, I've still got a few missing teeth from a boofhead who smacked me when he was on crystal meth. See, I went to this rollover. It was two Pommy blokes in one of them backpacker vans. No seatbelts. Nothing. They must've had a heap of drugs with them because, when I pulled up, Boofhead's mate took off into the bush to hide them. In doing so he'd left Boofhead lying out on the road. And this Boofhead feller proved to be nothing but trouble. To give you some idea, he looked like one of those soccer hooligans what cause all the strife at the Pommy soccer matches; even down to the Union Jack he had tattooed on his head.

Anyhow, he'd gone through the front windscreen and, amongst a lot of other things, he had an ear hanging off and one hand was half ripped off. And I mean, I was there to help him, but he was so pumped up on crystal meth that all he wanted to do was have a go at me. He was a really big bloke too, about six foot and built like the proverbial shithouse. And like, I'm a bit of a weedy sort of bloke. Anyhow, when he shaped up, I said, 'Feel free mate but, if you do, for all I care you can go and sit down under a tree and bleed to death.'

Then – *bang* – the prick smacked me in the mouth. So, very much against St John protocol, I whacked him back. And not even that stopped him. When the two coppers turned up, they settled things down a bit. But when Boofhead's mate walked back out of the bush, trying to look innocent, the coppers raced off to nab him. So, then there's another struggle. Anyhow, this boofhead feller was so violent that I couldn't get a dressing on either his head or his hand. And because the coppers were busy with his mate, they couldn't split up and it looked like I'd be stuck with him in the ambulance by myself. So when a car pulled up and a bloke got out and said, 'I'm a doctor. Can I help?'

I said, 'By gee, you can.'

When we eventually got Boofhead into the ambulance, he was still thrashing around. So much so that the next thing I did, which was very much against St John protocol, was to restrain him on the stretcher with those cable-ties that truckies use to tie their load down with. See, you're only supposed to restrain a patient with the belts they have on the ambulance stretcher. The thing is, they can easily work their way out of them. So I cable-tied Boofhead to the stretcher. And the doctor was all for it. Given the circumstances, he thought it was a good idea – 'a stroke of practical genius'. Then, after I'd cable-tied him, the bugger started spitting at me. 'Blow this,' I said and, also very much against St John protocol, I pressed a pillow over his head. And that slowed him down. See, you don't smother them. It just shuts their world off.

Anyhow, by the time we did our halfway changeover with Broome Ambulance, he'd snoozed off. Though, before I handed him over, I took the cable-ties off. Next day Broome Hospital rang me, 'Mick,' they said, 'did this Pommy feller try to commit suicide or something?'

I said, 'Why?'

They said, 'By the look of it, it looks like he's tried to slit his wrists.'

That was from the cable-ties being yanked so tight. I said, 'Gee, sorry fellers. Wouldn't have a clue. I can't really explain that one.'

I tell you, from all his thrashing around, it took half a day to clean up the blood that was splattered around the ambulance. Anyhow, that was one of my more difficult jobs and, like I said, I've still got a few missing teeth to prove it.

The Barber

(Swampy)

For the past couple of years I've attempted to cut my own hair. Obviously it hasn't worked. On a few occasions I have been likened to a, quote, 'middle-aged, balding, woolly mammoth'.

The thing is, I don't like modern-day hairdressers. They charge through the nose and you end up coming out like a carbon copy of some film star in a glossy magazine or, in my case, the diabolical resemblance of one. There's no way I want to look like Bruce Willis or Arnie Schwarzenegger or Clint Eastwood or even the great Chips Rafferty, God rest his soul: Give me the good old days when a proper barber gave you a fair dinkum haircut and charged next to nothing.

Well, just a couple of weeks ago, I stumbled upon a real barber, tucked away behind some shops. Here was the place for me. It took me back thirty or so years when Dad used to drive me all the way over to Temora just to get a haircut. There was an Ardath sign hanging from the shop front. A barber's pole giddied around outside the door. Odd assortments of pipes, cleaners, knives, razor blades and cigarettes, bleached by the sunlight, adorned the window front.

I was drawn inside like a child to a magic shop.

The old barber was happily singing away as he worked on an even older semi-bald bloke. But the thing was, the barber still plied his craft with the love and care he had for the past fifty years. He treated every one of those dozen or so hairs on the old bloke's head with respect, as if they were the most precious things on earth — which they probably were.

I sat down to wait my turn, wondering, with a wry, inward grin, if the barber had yet converted to decimal currency. Picking up the latest magazine off the small glass table, I read with interest how our missing prime minister Harold Holt had been kidnapped by a Russian submarine. The intriguing story continued along the lines that he was taken into the USSR, brainwashed, and was now working for the KGB.

The barber finished with the old semi-bald bloke. After a quick whisk over with the powder brush, he staggered back out into the twenty-first century. I bounced into the seat like a ten-year-old. It was leather, and worn by the comfort of generations of patrons.

'How'd you like it?' the barber asked in a booming, semi-operatic voice.

'Just a trim of the hair and beard, thanks,' I returned.

I relaxed back into my childhood memories. There was the smell of the leather seat, the aftershave, and baby powder still tickled my nostrils. I could see the jar of Brylcreem. And was that a bottle of Californian Poppy partially hidden behind the clean white hand towels and the powder jar?

The barber added to the old-time atmosphere by breaking out into a medley of songs that had been sung by the stars of Dad's era — people like Nat King Cole and Bing Crosby.

Taking a quick glance in the mirror to give the barber a smile of approval, I noticed that he was getting a bit too caught up in the songs and carried away with the scissors.

'Not too short,' I reminded him. He ignored me completely and merrily continued scissoring and singing.

I had a twinge of panic as I recalled arriving home from Temora, resembling a shorn sheep, how the breeze howled into places where it hadn't howled for a while — behind the ears, the back of the neck.

The barber by this stage was in full voice as he put down his scissors and grabbed his clippers.

I recoiled. 'Not too much off, mate.'

My words were drowned by his singing.

I began to wonder if anyone would recognise me after this little excursion. It was too late to walk out, one side done, the other disappearing rapidly.

At least it'll be cheap, I consoled myself.

Dad always used to say, 'Don't worry, son. It'll grow back.' I never did come to grips with the logic of that statement.

'Oh no!' The barber was sharpening his blade on the strap — lathering up the shaving brush!

'I don't want a bald ring around my neck.' I squirmed. 'Remember, I said I just wanted a trim.'

My head was snapped back and the lather applied around my throat. For months I'd been trying to learn the words to 'The Man from Ironbark'. Suddenly the whole eight verses sprang into mind, crystal-clear, as though I'd written them myself.

I gripped the barber's chair. The hot metal blade scored its way over my Adam's apple. Good God. One day looking like a woolly mammoth, the next a replica of a turkey.

Sighting the tatty barber's licence on the wall, I noticed it'd expired back in the mid-1960s. I gargled a protest, but the barber was building up to the crescendo of 'Unforgettable'.

He stopped, mid-line. 'Leave it dry, or do you want water on it?' he called out.

'Leave it. Leave it dry,' I pleaded.

He took up singing where he'd left off, but with extra vigour. Out came a bottle with a spray top. I was doused in a mist of sickly scented water. Out came the Brylcreem. A massive blob of grease landed on my head as if it'd fallen from the bum of a passing albatross. A comb was dragged through what little remained of my once flowing locks.

Finally the barber flung his arms wide open. I wasn't sure if it was in admiration of his own work or to signal the end of the song. He took a step back as if waiting for the curtain to drop and the applause to begin. I sat agog, staring at the total stranger in the mirror, who sat agog, staring back at me.

'That's it,' shouted the barber. I staggered to the counter. 'How much?' I asked.

The barber cupped his hand over his right ear and leant over the counter. 'You'll have to talk up, sonny. I'm a bit on the deaf side,' he called.

'*How much is that!*' I yelled back.

'Thirty dollars!' he shouted.

Blame it on COVID

(Great Australian Ambos Stories)

G'day, Swampy. Lindy here again. Remember Lindy and Brian, the grey nomads? Me the ex-high schoolteacher-cum-history buff and my husband Brian the retiree from our local council. Thanks for printing my last story 'Larry the Horse' in your collection of *Great Australian Volunteer Firies Stories*. I even heard you talking about it in one of the radio interviews you did about the book. So well done. Those volunteer firies really are a great lot of people.

Now, back when I was telling you about 'Larry the Horse', I may have mentioned how, no sooner had Brian and I arrived back home in country Victoria, so that Brian could go and see his specialist, than the COVID restrictions came in. And now, here we are, over a year later and we're still damn well stuck at home. And mark my words, this is not the end of it. In fact, I've recently heard on the radio that Melbourne's now the most locked-down city in the world. Of course, what compounds our particular having-to-stay-at-home problem is that, if Brian's not out on the road, travelling, he gets bored and tends to overdo things with his home brewing. So he's been suffering something chronic from gout.

Anyhow, all that aside, when last we spoke you said that you were looking for ambulance stories. So, while Brian was busy home brewing in the back shed, I decided to spend my spare time down at the local library doing some research. And as always seems to be the case, when you're busy looking for dramas far afield, the biggest ones happen right under your very own nose, don't they.

One evening when I came home from the library, there was

Brian down in his shed holding court to all his rowdy croquet mates. And by the sounds of it, they'd spent the entire day in there tasting Brian's homebrews. Anyhow, a few hours later, after I'd organised a taxi for the last one who'd rolled out of the shed, Brian came into the kitchen, full of smiles, expecting his dinner. I said, 'Brian, if you expect to come into this house in the state you're in and expect me to have your dinner all laid out on the table for you, you are a very much mistaken man.'

Of course, he then tried taking on that doe-eyed look that used to win me over, decades ago, back in our old courting days. But no: being much older and wiser as I am these days, there was no way I was going to fall for that old trick again. Instead, I told him flat that there'd be no dinner for him that night and, what's more, there was no way he should even entertain the idea of us going to bed together while he was smelling like a brewery. At hearing that he got into one of his usual little huffs. 'Suit yerself,' he said. Then, as he was leaving the kitchen, he added, 'I was planning ter sleep out in the shed anyway.' He had an old camp stretcher out there that he sometimes used during a critical stage of one of his fermentations.

'Well, that just suits me down to the ground too,' I replied.

So off he goes, half expecting me to call him back. But I didn't. Not this time. Instead, I made myself a cup of tea and I went and made myself comfortable in bed, reading yet another Bill 'Swampy' Marsh classic, *Great Australian Bush Funeral Stories*.

Anyhow, whenever Brian and I have these little tiffs, after he's slept it off, he usually arrives in our bedroom the next morning, looking contrite, with a cup of tea in hand, apologising for his behaviour. 'Sorry about last night, dear.' To which I'd say, 'That's all right, Brian, but you really should think about cutting back on the drinking.' To which he'd say, 'Yes, dear.'

So that's how it normally works. Then, after he gets me breakfast, I fuss over him a little bit before I head back to the library to carry on with my research. And knowing Brian as I do, he'd mull over the possibilities of cutting back on his drinking before he'll head back out to his shed to check on his latest home brew and have another tasting, just to see if things were ticking along okay.

So that's the pattern. But not on this particular morning. When I woke up, not a stir came from the kitchen. So I waited a while longer. But no, still no sound, no contrite Brian and no cup of tea. So I'm wondering, What's happened to Brian?

After I'd made my own cup of tea, I went down to the shed. 'Brian? Brian?' But no reply. I opened the door and that's when I saw him, lying flat out on the floor, beer kegs all over the place and blood everywhere. As I later found out, when he'd got up from his stretcher bed in the middle of the night to go to the toilet, he thought he was still in our house. So when he wandered off to the loo, he ended up tripping over the beer kegs, and down he'd come with one almighty crunch. And oh, hadn't he made a good job of it. So I gave him a bit of a shake. 'Brian, Brian, are you all right?' And from his garbled reply, it sounded like he wasn't quite sure.

So I rushed off back inside, grabbed the telephone and rang the emergency number. I said to the young man who answered the phone, 'Quick, my husband's had a fall in the back shed, he's badly injured himself, please send an ambulance immediately.'

After I'd given the young man our address, he said, 'Has he had his COVID vaccination yet?'

I said, 'Well, he was supposed to have his first shot last week but he couldn't make it because he was suffering from gout.'

'So why did he have gout?'

Now I had a funny feeling where all this might be leading, so I cut the young man short and I said, 'Look, this has nothing to do with his drinking. He's fallen over in his shed, and he's knocked himself out, and he's cut his head and there's blood everywhere. Can you please just send an ambulance to pick him up and get him to hospital where he can be treated?'

'And what was he doing in the shed at the time of his accident?'

By this stage, I was getting quite irate. I said, 'Well, what business is it of yours anyway?'

He said, 'We just need to get some details before we dispatch an ambulance.'

I said, 'Well, he was sleeping in his shed.'

He said, 'Why was that?' Then, before I could think of an acceptable reason, he asked, 'Is this a domestic violence issue that you're trying to report? If so, I can put you straight onto the police.'

I said, 'No, it is not a domestic issue. I just came home from the library and Brian had been out in his shed having one of his homebrew tastings with a few of his mates. When he came in for dinner I suggested that he might like to think about sleeping out in the shed for the night because of the state he was in.'

'And may I ask what sort of state he was in?'

'Well,' I said, 'he just may have had a few too many.'

'Was he violent toward you?'

I said, 'Brian? Violent? Don't be damn silly. Brian wouldn't hurt a flea.'

'Then were you violent toward him?'

Well, that was it. I can tell you, Swampy, I must admit that's when I snapped. 'Now you listen to me young man, I don't know what's going on in that sordid imagination of yours but, after having put up with my husband's habits for the past forty years, why would I suddenly want to turn around and try to bludgeon him to death in the back shed?' Then before he could get another word in I added, 'And what's more, Brian's been a good husband to me in his own sort of way. He's always provided for our family, even through the difficult years with our two boys. If Brian hadn't had flat feet and a dodgy hip he would've volunteered to serve his country and gone over to Vietnam to fight against the communists, which is a hell of a lot more than what you're likely to do, young man!'

And that did the trick. The young man on the other end of the telephone line hung up, and within minutes I heard the siren coming down our street. Then two well-mannered young people appeared at my front door, dressed in so much personal protection gear they looked like they were entering a nuclear zone. After having a quick look at Brian, they went and got one of those gurney things from their ambulance. Then they rolled it straight through the house, all over my brand new carpet, and down to the shed, and they loaded Brian onto it. Then they rolled him right back through the house again and out into the back of the ambulance. Then they were gone.

Later on, after I'd cleaned up the mess, I went to visit Brian. And there he was, bandaged to the hilt, sitting up in bed, looking bewildered. The doctor told me that Brian had had seventeen stitches in his forehead, he'd broken his nose and a few ribs, he was badly bruised and he was suffering from concussion, but his amnesia was only short lived.

So there you go. That's the drama we had. You'll be pleased to know that Brian's now back home and on the road to recovery. But the thing is – and here's the story – if it hadn't been for all these damn COVID restrictions, none of this would've happened. Brian and I would've been somewhere up in the far north, travelling around in our caravan, and everything would've been sunshine and roses.

Footnote 1 – At the time of writing this story there have been over six million recorded cases of COVID-19 in Australia with 7367 deaths. In the state of Victoria, 1,540,311 active cases have so far been recorded and 2998 deaths. By some measures, over the COVID pandemic, the city of Melbourne has spent more time in lockdown than any other city in the world.

Footnote 2 – If you're keen to give home brewing a crack, a beer kit's the best way to go. As far as the space required goes, it's something you can easily do in your kitchen. Though in my case, my dear wife kicked up such a stink about me taking over her precious kitchen, I'm now brewing in the quiet calm of my back shed.

The Telegram

(The Complete Book of Australian Flying Doctor Stories)

After I left school back in 1950 I spent a hell of a lot of time in the pastoral area out in the west of New South Wales. And around that time the Royal Flying Doctor Service incorporated an on-line radio service through its base in Broken Hill.

This particular service was greatly appreciated by the station people because they didn't get into town much and it gave them the chance to place orders for food or machinery parts or whatever. In actual fact, I reckon that about 90 per cent of station business was carried out that way, back in those days.

Now, aligned to this on-line radio service, the Flying Doctor base also ran what us station hands called 'Galah Sessions'. And these Galah Sessions were in part set up so that, after the business was concluded, the station women could have a good chat to each other and catch up on all the gossip and stuff. But also, there was some time set aside for urgent telegrams to be read over the air.

Anyway, most of us out on these stations used to listen in on the Galah Sessions whenever we could and then to the telegrams as they came through. Everyone used to do it. It was a bit of a lark. What's more, it sort of brightened up our day, hearing the gossip from different parts — who'd had a baby, who was crook, who'd died, who was getting married, and so forth. And also, you never knew when an urgent message might come through for yourself from family or whoever.

Anyway, at this particular time I was working out on the White Cliffs road at Koonawarra Station, just doing ordinary stock work and the like. And we were sitting around one morning listening to these telegrams being read out when we heard what I reckoned to be the daddy of the lot.

Apparently things weren't going too well for one particular family down in Tasmania and there was this telegram which was read over the air to a station hand out at Naryilco Station, in south-west Queensland. I forget the poor chap's name but, anyway, the message said it all and, what's more, with the minimum of words.

It read: DEAR (whatever his name was)
FATHER DEAD — TOM IN JAIL —
SEND TEN QUID.
LOVE
MOTHER

As Mad As

(Great Australian Railway Stories)

When I was about seventeen years old I started on the railways in Junee, working as a casual, shovelling coal. That was in 1939 and, in them days, when you shovelled down or level you got 11 pence ha'penny a ton but, when you threw it over your shoulder, it was a shilling a ton. Then I got on as a casual cleaner, cleaning the train engines, and eventually as cleaner. Oh, and I also done the call boy job around the town because I knew everybody. Calling was waking the drivers, the firemen and the guards up at whatever time of the day or night they wanted, to tell them what job they were doing. Some asked for half-an-hour's notice, others wanted an hour. It depended.

And in them days, God, in Junee alone there'd be dozens of call boys. See, there was four ordinary express trains of a night. Holiday time there'd be anything up to six or eight heading south to Albury and north to Sydney, then there'd be trains coming down from Narrandera and them places, out that way. So you might have to call forty to fifty men of a night. And well, the fireman, he could be living up one end of the bloody town and the driver might be up the other end. So you'd be going as flat as a tack from the time you got on the pushbike at eleven o'clock at night till your last call, say, around five or six in the morning. And there were some cranky blokes and there was some good blokes — same as usual.

But with the calling we had a lot of them cat's eyes. You know, the bindy, those prickle things with three sharp prongs. And they were bad. The bastards would puncture our tyres before we'd even gone 10 yards, if you gave them the chance. But we used to get a quarter of a cup of sugar and mix it to a paste with water then we'd suck it up into our bike pump and blow it into the tyres — just like the stuff they've got today for mending punctures — and that's what kept us out on the road.

Then, after Junee, I got on as a fireman and I went everywhere. But geez, some of them fellers used to drink, them days. Bloody hell, I remember one time carrying a drunk driver on me back from the Wagga railway station down to our loco with his false teeth clattering around in me pocket. Oh, I had to do the lot, then. I got the engine ready and I got the train out on the road — the track — while the driver just went to sleep on the floor with the diddy-box under his head. The diddy-box is the box with the detonators in it, in case you break down. So it would've given him one hell of a headache if the diddy-box had've blown up, eh.

Then another time with the drinking: see, there was a depot at Harden, a big barracks where all the fellers stayed over between trains, and it was a regular thing that, when you got to the barracks, you went down the pub for a few beers. Well, this particular night this train driver and his fireman, they had more than a few beers. They got stonkered, and around midnight they were on their way back to the barracks when they came across this rooster sitting on the fence.

'I'm feelin' hungry,' the driver said. 'Me too,' said the fireman.

So they got this bloody rooster by the scruff of the neck and they ringed it and they took him back to the railway barracks and they plucked him. And in the barracks, them days, they had those big coal ranges, so they stuck this rooster in a pot with some water and a bit of salt and pepper and they stuck it on this stove. Then, after an hour or so they opened up the tap at the bottom of the pot and they poured themselves a bit of soup and they reckon it was pretty good. Then an hour or so after that, into the barracks came a set of men from down the pub and the drunk fellers said, 'There's some soup in the pot there, have some.'

So these fellers go over and they fill up their mugs. Anyhow, after there's been about ten or so blokes had a go at this soup, these two blokes from Goulburn come in from off the job and they got a mug-ful and they're sitting by the stove drinking it and one of the drunk blokes said, 'How do yer reckon the soup's goin'?'

And the feller from Goulburn, he said, 'It's pretty good, only the barley could'a been cooked a bit longer.'

Then the drunk feller said, 'But we didn't put any barley in it.' And another feller asked, 'Did you gut the fowl?'

'No,' they said, 'we didn't know nothin' about that. We just stuck the whole bloody lot in the pot.'

So they'd been eating all the guts and the giblets and every bloody thing. So they must've been pretty drunk, eh.

Then there was a feller by the name of Drew. He wasn't drunk; this's just another story. Anyhow, Drewie used to drive the train from Macksville to Coffs Harbour, taking kids to school. Well, one time he got to the railway barracks at Coffs Harbour and he was having a cup of tea there and the cleaning lady come over and she said, 'Geez, Mr Drew, I'm havin' trouble with the cockroaches.'

'I'll tell yer what to do,' Drewie said. 'Make up a mix of sulphur and lard and when yer catch a cockroach, roll him on his back and gently rub it onto his belly. Sure as eggs, it'll kill him.'

Then the cleaning lady, she said, 'Geez, Mr Drew, wouldn't it be simpler to just squash 'em with yer foot?'

And Drewie had a bit of a think about it and he said, 'Yeah, well, I guess that's another way yer could go about it.'

Another story Drewie told us ... see, on the other side of Urunga there's a big steel bridge over the Bellinger River and at this time there was a mob of workmen sandblasting and repainting the bridge. Anyhow, all these schoolkids, they'd get on the train and they'd go to all the toilets and do their business but they wouldn't pull the chains. Then, just as the train hit the bridge, they'd pull the chains and *whoosh* it went all over the workmen. Drewie reckoned you could hear these fellers calling out from under the bridge, 'You little bastards!'

But I had all me bloody years on steam and, oh, they were great old days, and a lot of history, too. I remember I was in Junee when the 38-ers were running down there. I fired on them. Gee, they were a beautiful engine them big green fellers, the 38-ers.

But the railways are finished now. All the old blokes are disappearing and the humour's gone. Ever notice how nobody seems to laugh much these days? I used to have a bit of a laugh with one old mate from my railways days, but he's been put in a home down at Adamstown. He can't hear and he can't see, the poor old bugger. I used to fire for his dad and, when he come to Kempsey, he fired for me. Then there's another old railways bloke, he's been a mate of mine for sixty years now. He's near ninety but you wouldn't get much sense out of him. He's as mad as a shit-carter's horse.

A Drover's Wife

(Great Australian Droving Stories)

I didn't beat about the bush. I met the wife-to-be on the Saturday night and I asked her to marry me on the Sunday night. The only problem she could see about that was that I was still recovering from a tangle with a horse while I was out droving, and she reckoned we should wait until I got off my crutches.

But I just knew that there was something about her. And what's more, I knew she didn't want me for my money because she knew full well that I never had none. So that was in 1950, and it happened out at a place called Coolah, which is about a hundred and twenty or thirty mile north-east of Dubbo, there in central New South Wales.

Anyway, when I finally got off the crutches she still seemed keen on going through with it even though I was having a bit of trouble with the mother-in-law-to-be. I mean, we ended up good mates in the end but at that stage we weren't. Anyhow, I hadn't been home to see my folks in three years so naturally, they hadn't met the wife-to-be so I said to her, 'Do yer want'a meet my parents?'

'Okay,' she said.

Now my parents lived down south, down near the Victorian border, which was a long way away. So for the first stage of the journey we were all day and all night on the train until we got into Sydney at about five in the morning. Then with nothing better to do, when the shops were open, we got a taxi to drop us off up town so that we could have a look around. Anyway, we were walking past a Registry Office when I got this bright idea, see, so I very romantically said to the wife-to-be, 'How's about tying that figure eight knot that yer can't undo with yer teeth, right here and now!'

'Okay,' she said.

But then, when we asked in at the Registry Office they said that one of us had to live in the district. Now, the-wife-soon-to-be, she'd been on a holiday, visiting relatives, in the area about three years beforehand so she give them that address. So that was all right.

The next problem was that we had to have two witnesses and, what's more, they had to have known us for at least six months. That was a bit more difficult because we were in a bit of a rush and I was new to Sydney. Anyway, I was feeling a bit disappointed so we walked outside and three taxis were going past so I whistled one up and, oddly enough, the driver was the very same bloke that'd brought us up town. So I grabbed him and explained the situation and asked him if he wanted to be a witness at our wedding.

'Okay,' he said.

Then I said, Thanks, and also can yer dig up a mate to be a second witness and be back up to the Registry Office at about three this arvo.'

'Okay,' he said.

So that was fine. Then we went to buy the ring. Now the only problem there was that I couldn't spend over three quid because that's all the money I had. So in the end we ended up having to go to three or four different jewellery shops before they had any sort of decent ring I could afford.

Then at about three, the taxi driver turned up with one of his mates. And when the feller at the Registry Office asked them how long they'd known us they said, 'Oh, we're old mates.' 'Known each other fer ages,' they said, and that did the trick.

And what's more, they turned out to be pretty nice fellers, too, because they gave us a quid each for a wedding present. That was good money in them days. So then we had a piece of cake and a coffee for a wedding breakfast and at seven o'clock that night we jumped on the train again. Then we spent that night on the train and we got to my parents' place at about nine o'clock the next night.

Then after we got back from visiting my parents I took the wife back out droving with me. At that stage I was working with another chap and his wife — this was with sheep. The chap drove the truck and caravan, his wife did some cooking, and I had the horses and dogs.

But my wife, she turned out to be petrified of horses, just petrified. But she still helped out. She paid her way, all right. She'd get busy and she'd go ahead and help get the yards up and things like that for when I arrived with the sheep.

So that was that, and that's how she became a drover's wife. Then twenty-five years after that, I lost her. She died. But she done a good job to put up with me for that long, I reckon, so you could say that I had a honeymoon that lasted twenty-five years.

A Stitch in Time

(The Complete Book of Australian Flying Doctor Stories)

We were up at Mintabie one time, Mintabie being a small opal-mining town in the far north of South Australia. Anyway, we'd just finished doing a clinic there and we were about to pile into the car to go out to the airstrip when this ute came hurtling down the road.

'Oh, my God, something terrible's happened,' I mumbled.

'Obviously some disaster or other,' replied the doctor.

Anyway, somewhere among a cloud of dust and spitting gravel the ute skidded to a halt beside us, and out from the ute jumped this bloke. He was in a blind panic, we could see that, and he starts calling, 'You've gotta help me, doc. There's been a huge fight, an' Igor's had his chest cut open. There's blood an' guts everywhere.'

'Okay,' said the doctor. 'So where's Igor?'

'I brung him along,' this bloke replied, rushing around to the back of his vehicle. 'Here he is, right here in the back o' me ute.'

So we grabbed our medical gear and shot around to where the bloke was standing and there was Igor, all sprawled out on the floor, blood everywhere, his guts hanging out, just like the bloke had said.

'Oh, my God!' I gasped.

But it wasn't so much the sight of the blood and guts that made me gasp. What really did it was the mere sight of Igor himself. Because Igor turned out to be a dog. What's more, he wasn't your normal sort of average household mutt. Not on your life. Igor was absolutely huge, massive even, and without a doubt he was most surely the ugliest thing that'd ever been born into the dog kingdom.

And not only was Igor abnormally huge and abnormally ugly, he was also abnormally angry, more angry than I've ever seen a dog be angry. Even with his intestines spilling out all over the back floor of the ute, Igor still had enough anger in him to snap off your hand in one bite. No beg pardons. And that would've been no problem at all because he had teeth on him like walrus tusks which, in a subliminal flash, made me wonder just how big and angry the other dog might have been and just how ugly it might have looked, as well. That's the dog that caused so much damage to Igor, I'm talking about.

'But Igor's a dog,' I protested.

'Igor's more than a bloody dog,' the bloke replied. 'He's me bloody best mate. Got a heart o' gold, he has.'

'But we're from the Flying Doctor Service,' I said. 'We're not vets. We don't work on animals.'

'Fer Christ's sake,' spat the bloke, 'if'n yer can stitch up a bloody person, surely yer can stitch up a bloody dog.'

Now there was no way that I wanted to get within cooee of the brute, 'heart o' gold' or not. I'm not too keen on those sorts of dogs at the best of times and I made my feelings felt. But I could see that there was a flicker in the doctor's eye and I could see that he was of a different mind and, what's more, that at that very moment he was thinking along the lines of having a go at sewing Igor back together.

'Let's have a go,' he said.

There. I was right.

So, among much fear and trepidation we got the bloke to hold Igor still and I stuck a drip into him and gave him an anaesthetic. Then, when he was knocked out, away we went.

I tell you it was one of the quickest operations in the history of canine-kind. A electric sewing machine couldn't have done the job any faster. In a flash we'd stuffed Igor's stomach back up where it was supposed to go and the doctor was busy doing a frantic stitch-up job.

Then, just as the last stitch was completed and tied off, Igor started to come to. That was made obvious because he gave a guttural growl which shook the ute right down to its bald tyres.

'Let's get out of here,' I called.

So we did. We were in that car and out of there like greased lightning.

Learners

(Great Australian Shearing Stories)

There isn't too much that I haven't seen during my fifty years of shearing; all the droughts, all the floods, the blowflies, the lot. But back when I started, when I was fifteen, I was just a cocky shearer and I only shore for neighbours and the like. So I never travelled much until about 1980 and that's when I began to work as a shearing coach and instructor. Then after that I did get into some of the famous sheds; sheds like Funny Hill, over near Crookwell, in the south-east of New South Wales.

Now Funny Hill was also renowned as being a very tough shed inasmuch as they used to buy a lot of heavy-wooled sheep from places out west like Warren and Quambone. And when they came back to Crookwell from those drier places they were big and hungry and, as soon as you put them on the wet grass and better feed, they got a lot of extra wool grease which made them dynamite to shear. At times you just about had to chisel the fleece off.

Like, I was at Funny Hill one time, coaching these sixteen shearers — good, experienced, shearers they were too — and just three of them getting their hundred a day. Most were only shearing between 50 and 70. And I can tell you, these fellers were doing it very hard. And, what's more, they knew that there were still over 20,000 red-eyes, or wethers, ready to walk up the plank outside. Heartbreaking, it was.

It makes you wonder why some of these fellers want to shear in sheds like that. I mean, another time, one young learner said to me, 'Can you get me in to Funny Hill?' And I said, 'I can get you in alright but I'm not sure you'll ever get back out again.' Oh, it was a tough shed that one. A few reputations were made and lost there, I can tell you.

So, in all, I've coached around a couple of thousand blokes; blokes that could shear anywhere between 60 and 300 a day. And of course people say, 'Why would a bloke who can shear 300 a day want a coach?'

'Well, just look at Greg Norman,' I say. 'He wins a tournament and then he goes up to Charlie Earp and says, "Look Charlie, I missed three fairways the other day. I'm going bad. What do you reckon I can do to rectify the problem?"' And that's the thing, they just need to keep honing their technique if they want to stay up there with the best.

But no, I've been lucky. Just working as an instructor has given me the opportunity to travel. I've been from Mungindi, up on the Queensland border, to Berrigan down on the Murray River, south-east to places like Goulburn, north-east to Willow Tree and further up to Guyra, out west to Bourke, south-west to Hay. So I've covered a fair bit of the country. And over that time I've started almost nine hundred learner shearers and not all of them have been Aussies either. I've taught Chinese shearers, Polish shearers, Russian shearers — the lot.

But of course, being learners, they're always a good target for stories. I guess you've heard the one about the boss coming along to a learner shearer and complaining about the wool being left on the sheep's legs.

'Look,' says the boss to the learner, 'you can't let them go like that, they've still got wool all down their legs.'

And the learner looks up and says, 'But boss, they're little soldiers. I've left their gaiters on.'

'Well,' snaps the boss, 'that bugger over there must be the bloody sergeant because you've also left his hat on.'

Then there's another one where the boss walks past the learner and he's battling away trying to shear this big wether and it's kicking and kicking and knocking this young bloke about, and the boss says, 'Look son, put some wool in his mouth and let him chew on it. That'll keep him quiet, you'll see.'

So the boss goes off and does some penning up and when he comes back this feller's still on the same sheep and it's still kicking him all over the floor.

'Look,' says the boss, 'I thought I told you to put some wool in his mouth to keep him quiet.'

'I did, boss,' the learner says. 'But the bastard eats it faster than I can cut it off.'

Then another one's when the boss comes in and he says to the learner, 'Hey,' he says, 'you should've cleaned those bloody sheep up better, they've still got a lota wool on their legs.'

'But boss,' the learner replies, 'it's gonna be a bad year for snakes, so if there's still wool on their legs, they won't get bitten.'

And the boss says to the learner, 'Well, if you took a bit of bloody wool off their eyes they'd be able to see the bloody snakes!'

Cleanliness is Next To ...

(Swampy)

The Browns lived on a property about a mile out of Beckom. There were three in the family: Mrs Brown, her hen-pecked husband BBQ Bob, and their son (my mate), Brownie.

Mrs Brown's favourite saying was 'Cleanliness is next to godliness', which just about summed her up. Her house always looked as if it'd just been redecorated. Smoking was banned, not only from the house block, but the whole property. The lawns were cut and edged to perfection. Flowers forever bloomed in her garden. The chook pen was scrubbed and washed regularly with Dettol. So clean and perfect was it all that both BBQ Bob and Brownie felt uncomfortable living there, but such was their fate.

Even the visitors' dunny adorning the bottom of the backyard stood as a monument to this lady of cleanliness, with its bright brick red roof, its hi-glossed white walls and green Duluxed door upon which the mandatory *NO SMOKING* sign was stuck.

Spiders, snakes, mosquitoes, cockroaches and even flies were apprehensive about nearing the Browns' block. But alas, the ants took no heed and strode in where so many others dared not, to set up home in that glistening visitors' dunny.

The reason it was called the visitors' dunny was because, when BBQ Bob invited his friends over for one of his delicious BBQs, Mrs Brown wouldn't let anyone use the inside toilet for fear the house got dirtied. So, the visitors' dunny remained, and after many failed attempts at poisoning, so did the ants.

One evening, Mum, Dad and me were guests of the Browns for their twenty-fifth wedding anniversary. The beer flowed as freely as Mrs Brown would let it. The BBQ was its usual high standard. The crop was looking good as the weather had been kind. All in all, the Browns' twenty-fifth year was looking as well as any that'd preceded it. We all relaxed on the back verandah overlooking the manicured backyard and blooming garden, watching the sun set over the visitors' dunny. Even Mrs Brown seemed in good spirits as the first flicker of the evening star took to the sky.

But we all knew that BBQ Bob had been keeping a secret from his wife for those past twenty-five years, that being his enjoyment of the odd puff on a cigarette.

Mrs Brown's aversion to cigarette smoke verged on the paranoid. After BBQ Bob came in from burning off on the farm, or home from his allowed once a week visit to the pub, he was made to change his smoky clothes before entering the house. Little did Mrs Brown realise that the smoky smell was mostly of BBQ Bob's own doing.

So, when BBQ Bob excused himself with a wink in Dad's direction, we all knew what he was up to ... except Mrs Brown. Mum covered for BBQ Bob's temporary absence by taking up the conversation with Mrs Brown.

'Everything's looking as neat and tidy as ever, Jean.'

'Well, you know what they say: "Cleanliness is next to ..." By the way, did you happen to notice that I've finally got rid of those dreaded ants from the outside toilet?'

'I was wondering what the strange smell was,' Mum replied. 'Yes, well I just mixed up some old gunpowder with petrol from the lawn mow—'

A flash lit the evening sky.

The explosion that closely followed rocked the house's foundations.

Three galahs fell from above suffering heart attack.

The visitors' dunny's hi-glossed walls skipped gaily across the open paddock in slow motion. The brick red roof rocketed moonwards. The Duluxed door, with its mandatory *NO SMOKING* sign, took to the heavens, fluttering like a leaf before crashing back to earth, right in the middle of the flowering garden.

When we reached the site, BBQ Bob was still on the can. A fag-end hung from his swollen lips like an ignited firecracker. His clothes smouldering, face blackened, hair singed and frizzy. Even the toe caps were blown clean off his riding boots.

'CAUGHT!' was Mrs Brown's sympathetic greeting. 'I've finally caught you red-handed, Bob Brown!'

With help on its way, we discreetly excused ourselves and headed homeward. Well down the road, we could still hear Mrs Brown going off at BBQ Bob as he smouldered away on the can with second degree burns.

When we went to visit the poor bugger in hospital a few days later, he told us Mrs Brown was even more angry at him than ever.

It wasn't so much the smoking ... or even the damage he'd done. No! Even worse than that! Mrs Brown had discovered that the ants had returned to nest in the spot where the visitors' dunny used to stand.

Peas, Anyone?

(Great Australian Shearing Stories)

This story's through a child's eye, mine to be exact, and it happened when I was a little girl of around nine or ten when we were living at Gum Flat, at a place called Kalangadoo, in the south-east of South Australia.

Now, each season we only had about four or five shearers come to the property. And, with just that many, these shearers used to come up to the house for their main meals and Mum did all the cooking. So it's my guesstimate that the kitchen was about a hundred yards or so from the shearing shed, which seemed to be a hell of a long way, especially when you're just a wee person.

Anyway, on this particular day, Mum rang the bell to let the shearers know that lunch was ready. Then, after they'd washed, they all started trooping up to the house. Lunch was the usual, a roast with vegetables, the roast being lamb; mutton really, and the vegies were always potatoes, pumpkin, carrots, along with either peas or beans.

So, anyway, Mum rang the bell this day and these four or so shearers set off on their way up to the house. They were all skylarking about and giving one bloke in particular a hard time, scruffing him up a bit. It wasn't nasty or anything, just playful stuff. So there they were, they piled into the kitchen, sat down at the laminex table and Mum started to serve up their meal of roast mutton, potatoes, pumpkin, carrots and, on this day, she'd boiled up a stack of peas.

As usual, us kids were in the kitchen. We weren't eating with the shearers or anything. We were just hanging around, like kids do. Now it was a pretty hot day so these shearers just wore their usual boots, shorts, blue singlets, and around their necks they'd tied small towel types of things that were larger than handkerchiefs. They were there to absorb the sweat and to keep the shearers cool while they were doing the shearing.

Anyhow, while Mum was serving up their lunch, these shearers were still stirring this one feller up. But that all stopped when Mum had filled their plates with the food. And it was just as the shearer who was being stirred up by the others leant over his plate to reach out and grab the bowl of gravy, that us kids noticed a number of small ball-bearing-like things fall from the small towel around his neck. Out they came and fell straight onto his plate.

Now us kids couldn't believe our eyes because, for the life of us, these ball-bearing-shaped things looked for all money like sheep's pebbles, sheep's poo. But we weren't sure. We looked at Mum to see if she'd seen anything but she had her back turned. Then we looked at the other shearers but they'd turned away and were cackling themselves about something. But what really shocked us was that this feller hadn't noticed a thing because he grabbed the gravy, smothered his plate in the stuff, and he started wolfing into his meal like he hadn't had a decent feed for years.

So us kids, we just stood there with our mouths agape, our eyes agog, and our brains spinning around, thinking, 'Were they sheep's poo or weren't they sheep's poo?'

'And what's wrong with youse kids?' the shearer asked between great mouthfuls.

'Nothin',' we chorused.

And the feller went right on eating and when he'd finished he grabbed some bread and he got stuck in and mopped up the remaining leftover gravy and peas. So we're there, still thinking, 'Were they or weren't they? Surely not. Surely the other shearers wouldn't play a dirty trick on their mate like that. And if they did, surely the feller would be able to taste the difference between peas and sheep's poo, even if it was smothered in gravy.'

Then when his plate was as clean as a whistle the feller leaned back on his chair, real satisfied, and said, 'Beautiful missus, beautiful. Especially them peas,' he said. 'Yer done 'em exactly like me mother, just with a hint 'a mint in 'em.'

Now that sealed it because Mum never put mint in her peas.

Nicknames

(Great Australian Outback Trucking Stories)

G'day, mate. Sorry for the delay in getting back to you. But like I said the other day, I don't get much time to sit still these days because I'm mostly out on the road trying to scratch out a living. Like just now, I'm on my way down to Mount Gambier, in the south-east of South Australia. Hang on a tick; I'm just having a bit of a drag race with a bloke here. He's got a lighter load than me, so he overtakes me up the hills and I catch him up going down the other side and out of the flat.

Anyhow, I managed to have a chat with quite a few truckies — you know, fellers who've been around the traps for a lot longer that I have — and we've come up with a whole string of nicknames for you. In fact we had a real ball getting them together, and so did the wife, who sort of put them in some kind of theme-order for you. Some are fairly common, both inside of trucking and outside of trucking. Then there's some others that aren't so common. You might get a bit of a laugh out of those ones. But all of them have a story to tell about how they got their nickname. Oh, and there's probably a few that you mightn't be able to use in your book because they may not be appropriate; you know, like the censors or whoever might reckon they're a bit too rude.

Look, I've got a whole stack of them here. There's a truck stop coming up in just a k or so. I'll pull over there and read them out to you and you can use them as you like. Just hang on a tick.

Okay, are you ready? Good. Here goes. I don't know if you know or not, but we've got quite a few New Zealanders in the transport industry — you know, people from 'across the *dutch*' as they say — and I've managed to dig up some nicknames that we use for them. Like, there's your usual Kiwi, of course. But then there's also Cuz, Little Cuz, Big Cuz and Cuzzy Bro or just plain Bro. And then there's the variations of those, like Little Bro, Big Bro and Middle Bro. Then apart from the New Zealanders, there's heaps of Aussies with shortened names like your Davos, Bazzas, Dazzas, Mackas, Gazzas, Shazzas and so on.

Then there's the ones who got their nicknames because of what they look like. Like blokes with skinny legs usually get landed with Lucky, as in Lucky Legs, or just plain Chook. Moose was called Moose because he looked like one. Boofhead and Ugly were called that because they were. Wombat was a huge thickset sort of bloke, with a real hairy nose. Guts was Guts because he had the biggest beer belly you're ever likely to see. Smiley was a happy sort of bloke. Another trucking mate of mine told me about a small, thin feller that they'd named Sparrow or just plain Sproggy. Pigmy was apparently a short-arsed feller, not much taller that five foot. Mozzie was a squirt of a wiry feller, who was one of the most annoying arseholes you'd ever likely meet.

Of course, blokes who had white hair were usually landed with Snow or Snowy. Curly had curly hair, as did Frizz. Most of them who had red hair were landed with either Bluey or Rusty. Another truckie mate told me how they'd nicknamed another red-haired feller Fox, because he not only had red hair but he was a cunning bastard.

Norm was quite a common nickname that came up in my conversations. And that was for a few different reasons. First it was given to someone who was like Norm: remember the fat and lazy couch potato bloke in the old 'Life. Be in it' commercials on the telly? That's going back a few years now. Another time a truckie feller was called Norm because he was a bit like that gung-ho American army general, Stormin' Norman, from around the time of the Gulf War. Then there was Norm from Norman the Road Foreman. That one apparently came about because nothing happened on the road without Norm knowing about it.

Now here's a few that got their nicknames because of how they went about things. Like, Sparkles got his moniker because his truck was always immaculately clean. Repo was pretty similar. Repo's the name of a car polish and so Repo got his nickname because he was forever washing and polishing his truck. A feller called Turbo thought his workmates labelled him that because he always got the job done quickly and efficiently — though, in reality, they'd named him Turbo because he drove flat-strap, like a fucking idiot. Gearbox was called Gearbox because his mouth was always stuck in overdrive while his brain was stuck in neutral. Another bloke was just called Mate, because that's what he called everyone else: his workmates, his boss, the police officers, his dog, his truck; even his wife.

Now remember the character Mole in the book *Wind in the Willows*. One feller told me that they labelled a truckie bloke Mole because his eyesight was so crap that he was forever having bingles in his truck. On the other hand, fellers who loved to party and/or were big drinkers were often called names like Pisshead or just plain Pissy. And one feller who really hit the turps was known to everyone as Alco.

Then there was the feller they called General — he was apparently a bit of a control freak and he gave orders left, right and centre because he wanted to run the whole show. President was another feller like that and Digger came about because most of his family were in the army. Then another truckie feller got called Digger after he'd married the daughter of the boss of a very big trucking company — so he was likened to a gold-digger.

Then there were the ones who had different sorts of voices and that. Like Froggy had a deep croaky voice. Squeaky had a real high-pitched voice. Mumbles mumbled, so no one could understand him. There was a feller called Foreign because he came from Lithuania or somewhere and no one could understand a word he said, probably not even himself. Then there was a feller they named Lisp because he had one, and another feller was named Fart because he had the worst case of wind anyone had ever known.

I also managed to dig up a few nicknames with sexual innuendos. Are you ready for those? I mean you mightn't be able to use a couple of them. But anyway, one feller who always ranted on about sex and how randy he was got the name Rooster. Horny was called Horny because he was pretty similar in many ways to Rooster. Tear-'em-off got called that because, out the back of a roadhouse one night, he mustn't have been able to get a woman's knickers off because his mates heard him shouting out to her, 'Fer Christ's sake just tear 'em off!'. Oh, just on that, another feller got called Knickers because it was rumoured that he wore women's knickers all the time. Then one of my mates said he knew a truckie feller who got labelled with Oleander. He reckoned that that one came about after the truckie feller's wife caught him screwing the next-door neighbour under their oleander bush. And now I'll leave you with this one: Wanka was a single feller who lived by himself and had a massive collection of porn magazines.

Then there were the fellers who weren't too popular around the trucking industry. Grub stunk to high heaven because he rarely washed his clothes and hardly ever showered. There was Pong ... because he did. And — sorry about the unintentional pun — but when he kicked up a stink about being called Pong, we changed it to Ping; as in Ping Pong, and he didn't even realise it. There was also a feller, Scrubby, who was a real messy and untidy and dislikeable feller. Long-pockets was a complete tight-arse. Sook was a sulky sort of bloke who just moped around, whinging and whining about anything and everything. Bottom Drawer was full of shit, while Maggot wasn't only full of shit but they reckoned he'd eat just about anything. Then there was Crab. Crab was a real crawler; you know, he was always sucking up to the boss and that. Ferret was another real lowlife sort of feller. And one you probably won't be able to print was Ankles. Nobody around the yard liked Ankles and, what's more, Ankles didn't like anybody, so they called him Ankles because all the other truckies considered him to be three foot lower than an arsehole.

So now to some of the more aggressive and niggly types. They were given nicknames such as Sluggo, because he'd slug anyone at the drop of a hat. Rocket was a real bad-tempered sort who was likely to go off his head at any time. Basher was a real angry kind of feller too — everyone steered clear of him — and you'd never know what Bonkers would do because he was as mad as a meat axe. So that was a few of them sorts.

Then there were the ones whose nicknames came about because they were the opposite of what they were, if you catch my drift. You know, like fellers who were called Rowdy, Noisy or Riot were usually your very quiet, docile sorts and Killer was the most harmless bloke you were ever likely to meet. While Tiny was six foot six and weighed something like 160 kilograms.

Anyhow, just a couple of other nicknames I dug up: one feller was called Popeye — as in Popeye the Sailor from the old cartoons — because he smoked a pipe and loved his spinach. Then there was an old truckie, who'd been around for yonks. In fact he was like a father to many of us, so we just called him Pop, while some of the other older fellers we'd just call Uncle. Oh, and then there was Beanie. Beanie got his nickname because he wore a beanie all throughout both winter and summer. And I've got to mention another mate of mine who was labelled Scamp, and that's because he was always in strife and up to mischief. Actually I went to school with his younger brother who they called Little Scamp.

And lastly I've got written down here a feller who went by the name of Rifle. Rifle apparently landed his nickname because, if there was any trouble, he'd be off like a shot, out of there. Another feller, Tail-lights, was similar because, if there was any whiff of trouble, that's the last you'd see of him — his tail-lights, heading off, down the road, in the opposite direction.

Anyhow, mate, that's all I've got for the mo. I'll get in touch if I hear any other nicknames you might be interested in. Take care. Talk soon. Got to get back on the road and see if I can catch up with this feller before I get to Mount Gambier.

Elephant

(Great Australian Railway Stories)

I spent forty-two years with Victorian Railways and I've been retired twenty-one years. Hang on, that's wrong. My mind's a bit scratchy, these days. No, it'd be about twenty-five years since I retired. Something like that. Anyhow, I joined back in the late 1930s, when I was a lad, and I started sweeping platforms and cleaning toilets and all that and I rose through the ranks until I was made a stationmaster at the age of twenty-nine, and over my time I worked in about ten stations in all different parts around Victoria.

So I've done a lot and I've seen a lot, and something I've seen that I don't like is the way they've been closing so many of these railway lines and that, down. Why, here in Nhill there's no-one left to man the station and I don't think there's a manned station until Tailem Bend or Murray Bridge. All the signalling's gone automatic. These days there's this big switchboard thing at Ararat where they just turn the knobs and dials and it runs all the signals and tells the train drivers where to shunt and when to stop or to proceed, and it puts them on to No. 2 track, or wherever. And they're also in radio contact so they can ring the drivers and let them know when they're going to cross a train. Oh yes, she's all automatic these days.

See, they don't need people anymore. And that's something I don't like because, with the railways closing down, it also cut out a lot of the local jobs. It's no wonder that most of these country towns are in the doldrums. Well, just here in Nhill, the electricity commission closed their office and put off about six people. The post office has been privatised. There's no switchboard girls. And where they had about twelve fellers working in a gang, to fix up all the faults, now there's only two and there's more faults than there ever was. Then all the banks have amalgamated. It's a lot of people and that's everywhere.

See, back when I was with the railways, every country town I lived in, everything came to us by train: the groceries, the beer for the pub, the hospitals, chemist medicines, farm machinery, superphosphate, oil tankers, even the circus. Oh yes, I don't know about other states but here in Victoria, Wirth's Circus always travelled by train and, if there was enough room in the railway yards, they'd even hold the circus in there. That's true. When I was at Hamilton they held it right there in the railway yards, not far from the Grange Creek.

So anyhow, do you want to hear some stories about the circus and the railways? I've got three stories about elephants here. Are you ready? Okay, here we go. Well, the first story is that one of the elephants ate carrot fern — that's a weed — and it killed it. Yes, that's one story. Well, that's all there is to it. Carrot fern's poisonous, and the elephant ate it and it died. End of story.

The next elephant story happened when I was at Wycheproof. Wycheproof's another Mallee town. It's the only place in Victoria where the town's divided by the railway line, up the main street. Anyhow, one time, at Wycheproof, an elephant escaped from the circus and it took off and it knocked down these people's fence. Then it went into their back garden and trampled over everything — all their vegetables and their flowers — and it also knocked a full rainwater tank off the tank stand. So that's the second story.

Then there's a third one. Now, at Charlton — that's another place I worked at — Wirth's set up their circus next to the railway station, which was right near to the railway dam. Anyhow, it was as hot as hell so when one of the elephants saw the water, it broke its chains and it went straight into the dam for a drink and a wash and a muck around. The only trouble was that, when it was time for it to come out for the show, it wouldn't budge. I mean, they called out its name, but no. They offered it food, but no. They couldn't drag it out because it was too big, so that was no good. They couldn't use a stun gun or anything because if it was stunned it might've just gone 'flop' in the dam and drowned.

So they were stumped as to how to get this elephant out of the dam, see. Then one bright feller came up with an idea. He went and he got a really long electrical extension cord. Then he bared the wires of this extension cord at one end and he threw that end into the railway dam and the other end he went and he plugged into the power point over at the railway station. Anyway, when he shouted, 'Flick the switch!' a feller at the switchboard end turned the electricity on.

Now, I don't know if you've ever seen an elephant fly or not. Well, that day, I just about reckon I did. I tell you, that elephant, it squealed like buggery and it just about took off. And that's true, and that's how they got the elephant out of the railway dam. They gave him a bit of a charge, eh, by electrocuting the water. The only trouble was that, once the elephant shot out of the water, it still had its momentum up and it took off like greased lightning, straight past the circus tent, down the main street, and it was halfway to the next town before they even caught up with it.

The Governess

(Great Australian Bush Funeral Stories)

Do you remember me telling you, about five or six years ago, about how us kids did our primary schooling via School of the Air? That was when we were living on our station property which was about three hundred miles inland from Carnarvon, in Western Australia. To start with, Mum tried her best to supervise us kids but, when that got too much for her, she had to find us a governess. Usually the governess would stay in a bungalow, separate from us, and they'd come over to the main homestead for meals and for our lessons.

Over the years we had quite a few governesses come and go. I think that was because they had to be someone who was a) capable, b) extremely patient and c) a person who didn't mind the isolation. And seeing how most of them were city girls, pretty much straight out of high school, looking for a job and a bit of adventure, life on a remote station property, miles from anywhere, didn't suit them. And also, what probably mightn't have helped was that us kids — us boys in particular — quite often got up to a bit of mischief.

I fondly recall the time when the old pipes in the bathroom wall of the bungalow were replaced. Anyhow, the holes were never completely patched over and so we'd try and spy in on the governess. While we considered it to be an extracurricular biology lesson, that's not how the governess saw it. Neither did Dad. When she told him that we'd been peeking through into her bathroom, boy, didn't we get into strife.

By then we were thinking along the lines of how biology had the makings of a pretty exciting subject. We were about nine or ten. I could just reach the pedals of the old Land Rover, so I was already driving out around the property, checking on the windmills and things. Anyhow, there were some water pools out along the river system and when it was hot we'd invite whatever governess we had at the time to come along for a swim with us and we'd try and talk her into going in the water without her top on.

We'd also play a few pranks on them. I remember one occasion when we tied a kangaroo under the governess's bedsheets. When she went to get into bed that night, oh, there were screams, the works. She hit the roof. The kangaroo hit the roof. She took off in one direction. The kangaroo took off in another.

Other times we'd scare the living daylights out of them with the snakes we'd caught. And because there were graves scattered around the place from the former settlers, we'd always stir them up with gruesome horror stories about how their bungalow was haunted by ghosts.

So, for whatever reason, our governesses didn't seem to last too long. As I said, they were pretty much city girls to start with and so the isolation could've been a big problem. Though I do remember one girl who'd come off a farm; she was a bit more adaptable and resilient than the others. Mind you, she did get caught up in a prank of Dad's.

We had a young jackaroo working for us by the name of John. John and another jackaroo were racing their motorbikes out to a muster. We'd had some pretty heavy rains come through and the roads had been washed out in a few places. In those days, occupational health and safety was the last thing anyone thought about, so they weren't wearing helmets. Anyhow, John was going flat out and he hit a washout and he was thrown off his bike. Over he went and, when he came down, he whacked his head on a rock and knocked himself out.

He wasn't too good, though by the time they got him back to the homestead he'd regained consciousness. It was going to be an hour or so until the flying doctor's plane could get to us, so Dad gave him some drugs and a couple of whiskeys to help dull the pain. Now, what'd happened was, when he'd hit his head on the rock, the top part of his skull had mostly come off. So it was flapping around and when you lifted it up, you could see his brain. Luckily the meninges wasn't broken because, if it had, he would've been cactus.

Anyhow, our lessons were soon forgotten and we all gathered in the kitchen, either trying to help or just to have a look. Dad then got our governess — the one with the farming background — to run outside and get some bandages and so forth. So while John was sitting on a kitchen chair with the top of his head off, Dad said, 'Look, when the governess comes back in, kick your leg out when I give you a tap on the shoulder.'

'Okay,' says John.

So when the governess comes back into the kitchen, there's Dad, he's got a fork and he's making out that he's lifted the top of John's head off and he's poking around inside his brain. At just the sight of it, the governess went as white as a sheet. But then, when Dad tapped on John's shoulder and he kicked his leg out, that was it. She fainted. Down she went. *Crunch.* So now we had two people with cuts on their heads, though, of course, one was more severe than the other. Anyhow, all ended well. The flying doctor arrived and they took John away and eventually he came back out to us as good as gold.

I remember another time when our lessons came to an abrupt halt. We had an old retired pensioner who'd potter around the place doing odd jobs like gardening and that. He would've been in his seventies. I'm not sure what his history was, but he'd been around a long time. That's all I know about him, but he was your typical old-timer of the area. He'd given himself a tough time. As soon as he got paid he'd go into town and set himself up in the pub and he'd stay there until all the money had gone. Then he'd come back out to sober up and, when he'd earned some more money, off he'd go back into town again. And that's how he lived, so his body would've been fairly well pickled to start with.

Anyhow, one time this old feller went missing. So lessons stopped while Mum grabs us kids and our new governess and we all go looking for him. Eventually Mum found him in the outside toilet. He was dead. Cactus. Pants down around his ankles and he had an extremely pained expression on his face. We found out later that he'd been constipated for some time and he'd gone to the toilet, sat down, and he'd exerted himself a bit too much and he'd had a heart attack. Apparently that's quite common with older people. So beware.

Anyway, Mum asked the governess to help her get this old feller out of the dunny. The thing was, by then, rigor mortis had set in and the poor old feller was pretty much set in his ways, sitting on the toilet. So Mum and the governess had to somehow extricate him out of the toilet and down a set of steps, to get him into the homestead, ready for the police to come and pick him up. Trouble was, he was quite a huge person and, with having rigor mortis, he was as stiff as a board, stuck in his upright sitting position.

We could see that the governess was a bit wary about it all. Being a city girl, I doubt if she'd ever seen anything that was dead, least of all an almost naked, aging male. Anyhow, they managed to get him off the loo but, because of his weight, and his rigid, awkward position, no matter how much they pushed and pulled, shoved, grunted and groaned, they couldn't get him out of the close confines of the toilet. So to save knocking him about any further, Mum decided that they should roll him up in a blanket. So Mum and the governess eventually jiggered this poor old feller around so that they could wrap him up in the blanket. Then, with a fair amount of effort, they finally managed to drag him out of the toilet. By now the governess was looking decidedly green around the gills.

Anyhow, as they were taking the old bloke down the steps, they dropped the poor bugger, and so out from the blanket appeared this stiffened corpse. In doing so, the old feller let forth an animalistic groan which in turn released his bowels. And oh, what a mess he made.

Of course, Mum being Mum, she burst out into hysterical laughter. But not so the governess. That was it for her. As I remember it, she didn't even bother to hang around for the funeral. She handed in her notice that afternoon and left on the mail truck the following day.

Dennis the Menace

(Great Australian Railway Stories)

I'm coming up to seventy six and I'm determined to continue to make everyone's life miserable for at least another twenty-four years. That's my goal. Anyway, I was born in Adelaide and we went to live out on the east–west railway line, virtually straightaway. My father was a ganger, in charge of a maintenance gang, on the Nullarbor. So we went out to what they call the old 298 Mile, just out of Tarcoola. We were there for a few years, then we went to Zanthus. That's where I went to school. A lot of people say to me, 'Hey, Alf, where did yer go to school?'

So I puff out me chest and I say, 'Zanthus Tech.'

'Oh, geez,' they say, 'you must'a had a good education, then.'

See, they don't realise that Zanthus was a little bloody town, out in the middle of nowhere. It's exactly 137 miles east of Kalgoorlie and, I might add, it's the prettiest little railway siding on the east–west line, big gum trees, the lot. Now, I'm not sure how many people would've been living there back then. I'm talking about the early 1940s, you know. But I do know that there were seventeen of us kids at the school; though, in saying that, you've got to remember that some of the families had five or six children. And the whole time we were there, apart from your usual sorts of scraps, there was never any big arguments, neither family arguments nor between us kids. Us kids mucked about amongst ourselves very happily. We even went out and played with the kids from Cundeelee Aboriginal Mission, which was about 25 miles north, and they also came in and we all played together. There was never any problems. But I always loved trains, right from back when I can remember, and at Zanthus they used to do a bit of shunting — you know, water, general, whatever — and the crews always gave us kids a ride on the train around the triangle. They'd show us how to fire and all that. Oh, they were wonderful. Though there was one incident, I might as well tell you. You know how there's always some little 'Dennis the Menace' in every place. Well, that was me. And out of the seventeen of us kids that were at school in Zanthus, there was one particular mate of mine, Donny Mitchell. Now, Donny was a bit of a Dennis the Menace, too. We were both about eight and, if anything happened in the camp, we'd be the first ones to face court. What's more, more often than not, we were usually found guilty as charged.

Anyhow, on this particular occasion a bullion train stopped at Zanthus on its way through. Old Kiwi Walters was the stationmaster back then. Of course, every train that came through was an occasion. But, with this being a bullion train, it was an even bigger occasion than normal. Of course, all us kids went down there to see this train. There were three or four armed guards hanging about on the platform, which was exciting, so me and Donny, we started asking them about what sort of guns they had, and how much bullion was on the train, and had they ever been robbed, and how many robbers they'd shot dead and all that. So they were sitting there with their guns, very relaxed, chatting away to us and I had a thought, so I said to Donny, 'Donny, come with me.'

'Okay,' he said and so we went down to what was called the 'trolley shed'. The trolley shed was where my father kept all the maintenance gear, and he kept his section car, and also that's where he kept his detonators; you know, those explosive things they used as warning devices on the railways.

So Donny and me, we got four detonators and we went back to the train. But instead of going up the platform side, we crept along the other side of the train — the blind side, where nobody could see us. Then we placed these detonators under the wheels of the bullion train. Next thing, the guard blows his whistle and gives the right-of-way and the train starts to move. Then, *Bang! Bang! Bang! Bang!* Off go these detonators. Then the train screeched to a halt, and, bloody hell, I didn't realise there were so many armed guards looking after that bullion. There were blokes coming out of windows, blokes coming out of doors. Guns were aimed left, right and centre, and poor old Kiwi Walters, the stationmaster, shot out of his office so fast that he banged himself on the door and nearly broke his bloody arm.

'Blimey,' I said to Donny, 'we'd better get out'a here.'

See, I just thought it'd be all a bit of a joke and that these armed guard fellers would know the difference between an exploding detonator and a hold-up gun. But apparently they didn't. So Donny and me, we took off. Then, after the train finally left, they did a round-up of all the kids and there were two missing, me and Donny, and that's how they found out who the culprits were.

Anyhow, my father was a very strict man so I got a hell of a hiding and I was sent to bed without dinner. But then, later that night, I heard all the men talking over a few beers in our kitchen and, oh, they were laughing and going on. Oh, they just thought it was a hell of a joke.

Go Away Back

(Great Australian Droving Stories)

I'll tell you just how good them border collies are. I'd been
away out the back country at a place called Coombie Station.
Coombie's out the other side of the Lachlan River, there in south-
western New South Wales. From Griffith you go to Hillston then
you go out behind Rota and, if you're lucky, you'll find Coombie
Station.

Anyhow out that way they moved a hell of a lot of sheep
around the place. But the manager bloke at Coombie had a
border collie. And that dog was held in such high regard by the
manager that, when it wasn't working, it'd ride around, not in
the back of the Land Rover ute, like you'd expect, but right up
there in the front, sitting beside the bloke himself.

I remember one time when it was pouring down with rain and
a bloke said to this manager, 'Can yer give me a ride?'

'Yeah,' said the manager, 'hop in the back.'

Well you should've seen the look on that bloke's face. 'Hang
on a tick,' he said. 'How's about I hop in the front out'a the rain
and the dog gets in the back.·

'Not on yer life,' said the manager bloke. 'That dog rides up
front with me.'

So there, that's how highly he thought of his dog. Anyhow a
few days later I was working some sheep and the same manager
bloke arrived with his border collie and he said, 'I'll take a few of
these wethers up to the house fer killers.'

'That's fine by me,' I said.

Then he said, 'Look, I want to see you up at the house, about some business. Jump in the Land Rover and the dog'll take care of the sheep.'

So we drove back about six mile to the house and we were sitting around on the verandah talking business and I happened to say, 'How long'll the dog be?'

'Oh, yer don't have to worry about that dog,' he said. 'It's coming.'

Well, it wasn't that long before the border collie appeared with these wethers. And I don't think the bloke had spoken one word to the dog. He didn't need to. It just knew what it was supposed to do. So anyway, when the dog got nearer the house, the manager bloke, he just walked over to the gate and he opened it. And that dog wandered up with those sheep and took them right through the gate and up to the yard. Like, you wouldn't find two dogs in Australia who could do that.

Oh, them border collies, they're amazing.

Then I had another experience with a border collie. It was a while after when I went out droving with a bloke. Then there was also an old feller. I forget who he was, just now. Oh that's right, he was me father-in-law! Blimey, how could I forget that! Anyhow, me father-in-law had a border collie that he wasn't using and when they haven't got any work they get bored and go a bit ratty, which was what this particular dog had done. He was still only a pup like, about eighteen months. Anyhow the father-in-law said to me, 'Look, this dog's never done no work so take it with yer and see if yer can get a bit'a brains into it.'

Anyhow off we went droving a mob of wethers; the drover bloke, the dog and me. And I just forget where we were, but this night the bloke who was droving with me, well, he woke up and all the wethers had taken off. So he woke me up.

'All the fuckin' sheep've gone!' he said.

So anyhow, I let the father-in-law's border collie go, like. And as you do, I said to the dog, 'Go away back.' And that dog, like

I said he hadn't had any training but he was off like a shot, off into the dark. 'Well, here's a go,' I said to meself. This's gonna be interesting.'

This's all around midnight, like, and the dog'd taken off. So I saddled up me horse and I hopped onto it and I trotted and I trotted. Then just on daylight I caught up with the dog and he was bringing the mob of wethers back. And like I said, that border collie pup hadn't had any training whatsoever.

'Well,' I said to meself, 'if I never.'

So at that point, I wanted to see just how good this dog of me father-in-law's was, so I went up the back of the mob and checked their tracks. And that dog'd got them in so tight that he'd kept them right on the track, right along the stock route fence line, like. And what's more, he'd got the whole lot of them; the whole bloody lot. Oh, I tell you he was just a born, natural worker. No doubt about it. So then I just sat back on the horse and I took it easy and that dog ... well, he brought that mob of sheep right back to camp.

Like I said, them border collies, they're unreal.

Takes Two

(Great Australian Railway Stories)

When I was twenty I went to see the inspector in Mareeba and he gave me a job up at Lappa Junction working as a fettler in a four-man gang. There was three of us Aboriginal, three out of four. The accommodation was quarters, with three rooms. Then I transferred to a five-man gang at Almaden, on the maintenance section. I was the only Aborigine. There was none of that friction. We all got on well. At Almaden the accommodation was a bond-wood hut. On both sides was a verandah and in the middle was a stove for cooking.

Both Lappa and Almaden are west of Cairns. The rail track branches at Almaden. One line goes up to Chillagoe, to the end of the Mungana Stock Route. The other one goes out to Forsayth to meet the stock coming in from the Gulf.

Then from those ganger days I went to a fourteen-man flying gang. Mareeba was our home depot, and we worked from Cairns to Almaden. We did that heavy work, laying down rails and sleepers and all that stuff. We were nearly all Aboriginal, you know, just with a couple of white fellers. One was an Italian feller. I don't know how he got there. But when I was in the flying gang we was working at Redlynch one day. It was raining and when it rains we don't go out unless there's an emergency. It was smoko time, so this Jason went over to a little shop, across the road, for a packet of wholemeal biscuits and when he came back he opened it up and there was all these weevils in it.

'Look,' he said, 'these biscuits are full of weasels.'

And he wondered what we was laughing for. Then we tell him that weasels are big animals so they couldn't live in a biscuit.

Then later on there was another feller, Kevin. His job was to travel out on the trolley and fill the graphite grease pots between Redlynch and Mareeba. The pots was a little tank on the inside of the rail, and the train wheels pick the grease up off the rail and it stops the friction on the curves. But this Kevin had a thing about snakes. He hated snakes. Worse still, he thought that snakes hated him, too; that they was all out to get him. One day he was travelling from Koah to Kuranda, through the Barron Gorge, and he saw this taipan snake between the tracks. He panicked and he opened the throttle of his trolley, flat out, and kicked up his legs as he ran over where this snake was so it wouldn't jump up and bite him.

Then as soon as he passed over the snake he took a look back. But he didn't see anything. No snake or nothing. Then he started thinking that the snake must be under the trolley and it was going to get him from there. That really got him scared so, while the trolley was going flat out, he jumped off into the bush. He didn't knock the rope off or put on the brakes or nothing. But when he jumps off, he then thinks, 'Oh, what've I done now? I'm gonna cause an accident.' Because the trolley was disappearing down the track at a rapid rate without him.

So, he decided to run back to where he'd passed a fettler gang, just before he saw the taipan snake. So, he starts running back and he comes around the corner and there's the taipan snake lying in the track. But see, he doesn't know if it's dead or alive and he wasn't going to get close enough to find out, so he gets another fright. So then he has to run up through the bush, around the snake, and all the time he's thinking that the bush is full of snakes, ready to get him. Anyhow, he finally gets back to the gang and they ring through to the stationmaster in Kuranda and he goes out and he puts a sleeper across the track to stop the trolley as it flies through the station. But that gave Kevin a big fright, that day.

But, oh, they were good days. I stayed there a fair time, till about 1981, and now I'm an Aboriginal worker with the Seventh Day Adventists. That's good, too. My area is from Sydney all the way to the tip of Cape York, so you see some rewards. You see some good change in people's lives. I've got a positive outlook for the future, between black and white. If we work together we will change the community. If we don't, nothing will happen. It takes two.

Snakes Alive!

(The Complete Book of Australian Flying Doctor Stories)

There was one poor feller who lived out near Lake Stewart, up in the far north-western corner of New South Wales.

Anyway, it was a very hot night. The moon was full. As bright as a street lamp, it was. This feller and his wife were sleeping outside in the hopes of catching any breeze that might happen to drift by. During the night he rolled over, and that's when he felt something scratch his back, razor sharp it was. Initially, he thought it was the cat but, when he turned over to shoo the thing away, he made out the deadly form of a snake slithering off in the direction of the chooks' coop. So he dashed inside, got his shotgun, charged back outside, and started firing into the chooks' coop in an attempt to kill the snake before it got away.

Of course, all this noise woke his wife. When she saw her husband blasting away into the chooks' coop, with her precious hens flying left, right and centre, and him calling out, 'I'll get yer, yer dirty bastard!', she drew the conclusion that the poor bloke had finally cracked. He hadn't been himself lately. What with the extreme isolation, the extreme heat, the extremely full moon, and the extremities of their current economic concerns — all these things had eventually caused him to go off his rocker.

So there was this chap's wife telling him off, yelling at him to stop slaughtering her chooks, and him still blasting away, mumbling something about how he was trying to kill a snake that'd just bitten him.

'Well, where's the snake then?' she shouted.

He stopped firing and when the dust had settled they peered through the moonlight. No sign of a snake. So he showed her his back. The wife took a look and saw a couple of deep scratch marks.

'You've been scratched by the cat,' she said.

'It were a snake,' he replied.

'A cat,' she said.

'A snake,' he replied.

This went on for a while, with his wife arguing that he'd been scratched by the cat which, in turn, had caused him to lose his marbles and shoot up her chooks, and him declaring that he was in full control of his marbles and that a snake had bitten him and, what's more, he'd seen it slither into the chooks' coop which was why he was shooting in that direction.

With both of them finally agreeing to disagree, he put in a call to the Flying Doctor. The doctor advised that the best thing for him to do was to drive into Tibooburra and get the nurse to have a look. 'Okay,' he said and he headed off to Tibooburra, leaving his wife behind to tally up the dead in her chooks' coop.

But his troubles didn't stop there. By the time the chap got to Tibooburra the snake venom had started to take effect. So when the nurse was disturbed at some ungodly hour by a bloke with a very slurry voice banging on her door, she assumed that he was drunk. It'd happened before. Blokes getting a skinful and knocking on her door. Usually, they weren't too much of a problem. All she had to do was tell them to get lost and they'd wander off, most of the time not knowing what they'd done in the sober light of day.

But this drunk was different. No matter how many times she told him to get lost, he still wouldn't budge from her door. Then when the chap started ranting and raving about how he needed to see the nurse because his wife didn't understand him, she rang the police.

So before the chap knew it, he was being apprehended.

'Yer got it all wrong. I've been bit b' a snake,' he protested groggily.

'That's the best one I've heard in a long time,' replied the policeman.

While all this kerfuffle was going on, the doctor had been attempting to get through to let the nurse know that the chap coming in from Lake Stewart had a suspected snake bite, and could she keep him under close observation. The problem was that the nurse didn't hear the call. It was only after the chap had been carted off that the doctor made contact. Yet, even then, the nurse didn't twig. In fact, during the conversation she complained to the doctor about the hell of a night she was having. How it was as hot as Hades and then, just as she had finally got to sleep, some drunk started banging on her door and she'd had to call the police to come and cart him off.

Anyway, the chap went from bad to worse during the night which caused everyone to reassess his situation and he was flown to hospital the next day.

Nearly died, he did.

Parrot

(Great Australian Shearing Stories)

If you're talking about loose cannons in the shearing game then you'll have to mention Parrot. Now, why he got the name of Parrot was because he had an undershot jaw and a big, hooked nose which made him look pretty much like a parrot. A Longreach bloke he was, from out there in south-western Queensland.

But by gee, he was a strange one, I can tell you. A real strange one. You just didn't know what he was going to do next. You did not have a clue. And he was a real argumentative bastard, too, he was. By God, he could argue.

Like, this Parrot feller took up golf one time and he got real passionate about it. He even talked the local club into paying for a professional golfer to come out, all the way from Brisbane, to instruct everyone on the finer points of the game, which meant himself in particular. So, what did Parrot do? From the moment this pro arrived, Parrot started arguing with him, telling him that every move he made was wrong. The bastard took over the whole show and he started going on about how there was something wrong with this pro's swing. Then there was something wrong with the pro's grip. Then there was something wrong with his stance and so forth. Got right up this pro's nose, good and proper, he did. But that was Parrot, he got up everyone's nose.

But it didn't deter the bastard. He loved his golf. Wherever he went, he always took along his golf clubs — shearing, shopping, to the pub, the lot. Everywhere.

So this time he went out shearing with one of Arty Swan's crews, out Stonehenge way. Arty was the contractor, like.

Well, this team of fellers left in the car late one night. They were all pretty pissed to start with, but then, halfway out from Longreach, Parrot gets into an argument with these blokes. I don't know what it was about, but anyhow they have this almighty blue, right. Any rate, at one stage they got out to relieve themselves — have a piss, like — and Parrot's still having a blue with this shearer and they ended up having a scrap, right there on the track, out in the middle of bloody nowhere. So they're having this stoush when Parrot spits the dummy.

'Yer all a pack a bastards,' he says. 'Get stuffed. I'm not goin' shearing with youse blokes or any other of Arty Swan's mob.' Then he grabs his golf clubs, his shearing gear, and the flagon of port out of the car and he starts marching back along the road to Longreach.

'Well, piss off, then,' the shearers called out and they hopped back into the car and off they went, out to this shed, leaving Parrot behind.

Anyway, the next day Parrot's still out there, making his way back to Longreach when a shearing overseer by the name of Stumpy the Cunt comes by. That's true. That's what he always introduced himself as. He'd say, 'Me name's Stumpy the Cunt. Cunt b' name and cunt b' nature.' Which was a pretty honest appraisal of himself, too, I might add.

So Stumpy comes along and there's Parrot practising his golf down this dirt road, away out in the middle of bloody nowhere. Now, this Stumpy's looking for shearers to work in a shed further out, see, so he sees Parrot practising his golf and, more importantly, he also notices that Parrot's got his shearing gear with him.

'What're yer doin'?' Stumpy says.

'Oh, that Arty Swan 'n his mob, I'm not gonna work with that packa bastards no more,' Parrot replies.

'Well,' says Stumpy, 'I got a pen that needs fillin', come 'n work with me.'

'Okay,' says Parrot, and he hops in the ute with Stumpy.

So Parrot's been out at this shed with Stumpy all week, but he hasn't told anyone, see. Nobody else knows where he is. So it comes Friday afternoon and Parrot's missus fronts up to Arty Swan's office, in at Longreach, to pick up her hubby's pay. And, of course, Arty's pretty burred up about all this and he says to Parrot's missus, 'That little arsehole,' he says. 'He went 'n had a blue with me shearers 'n he buggered off out on the road to Stonehenge 'n no one knows where he is.'

So Parrot's missus gets all worried about this and she gets Arty to call the police and a big search party's organised to go out and look for Parrot. Of course, by this stage everyone's thinking along the lines of how Parrot's wandered off, and he's out in the bush somewhere with his golf sticks, either dead or perished. Even his wife had given him up for lost.

Now, meanwhile, back at the other shed, Stumpy didn't have a clue what was going on. Of course, Parrot hadn't bothered to tell him anything. He'd told him bugger-all. And what's more, communication with Longreach was pretty slapdash. So the news somehow reaches Stumpy's shed that some shearer-or-other's gone missing and they're calling for people to join in and help in the search party, out on the Stonehenge Road.

So Stumpy calls for volunteers and Parrot's one of the first to put his hand up.

'Count me in,' Parrot says. 'I were almost lost out there just recently, meself,' he says.

So, off they all go to meet up with this search party, the one that's about to go looking for this missing shearer or whatever. So Stumpy, Parrot and the mob get to this prearranged spot out on the Stonehenge Road and there they all are, the police, Arty Swan's mob, the shearers, everyone, all just about to get this search under way.

So Stumpy's ute pulls up and Parrot sticks his beak out of the window. 'Who yer lookin' fer?' he asks.

'We're lookin' fer you, yer fuckin' arsehole,' they said.

So they called the search off. Lost a couple of day's shearing, they did. And, I tell you, Parrot wasn't the most popular bloke around the sheds there for a good while after that. Well, to be honest, he was never popular amongst any of us shearers at all. He just got on everyone's goat too much. Drove them crazy, he did.

But, I mean, Parrot was like that. Like I said, you couldn't rely on him. No one could. And you couldn't trust him as far as you could kick him. Not even his missus.

Another time, he came home from shearing; it was a Friday, so his missus said, 'There's not much to eat in the house,' she said, 'so how's about yer go down to the shop 'n get us some fish 'n chips?'

'Okay,' he says.

So Parrot gets his wallet, grabs his golf clubs, and he heads off down the street. But he didn't stop at the fish and chip shop like his missus had asked him to. No, he went right on by, straight out to the airport, hopped on a plane, and he went to Brisbane to play golf for the weekend.

So there's another bloody search on.

But, like I said, that Parrot was a real loose cannon; just one of those people that you didn't know what he was going to do next. A real fair dinkum arsehole.

Once Bitten, Twice Shy

(The Complete Book of Australian Flying Doctor Stories)

I reckon it must have been about four, or half-past four, on a Sunday morning. I was still in bed for some unknown reason. Anyway, the telephone rang. It was Big Joe McCraddok, the police sergeant from Birdsville. Mind you, I've changed names and locations here to protect the guilty.

'Come quick. Come quick,' Joe called.

'Why, Joe?' I replied. 'What's the matter?'

'Roota Kozlowski's been bit b' a snake,' he said. 'Roota Kozlowski's been bit b' a snake.'

Now you'd be able to imagine the sort of character Roota Kozlowski was, just from his nickname, but maybe you haven't heard about Big Joe McCraddok. He's quite famous around these parts. A real true-blue bush character. They did an article on him in one of those monthly magazines, a while back. The locals really gave him a stirring about that, especially the way he was posing outside the pub, in his uniform and all. Anyway, that's the media for you. Because, believe me, Big Joe's nothing like that. He's as male as they come; a real man's man, through and through.

'What symptoms has Roota got?' I asked.

'I don't know,' Joe said. 'He's still about half an hour out of town but he's on his way in so, if you come now, you'll be here just that much quicker.'

That sent me into a spin. I mean, Joe of all people knows that it takes time to organise the plane and everything, and there he was expecting me to be in Birdsville at a moment's notice.

'Look, Joe, you'll have to give Roota first aid yourself,' I said. 'I won't be able to get there within half an hour, you know that.'

'Oh,' came the disappointed reply. 'Must I?'

'You've done it plenty of times before,' I said. 'All you've got to do is to apply pressure immobilisation on him the moment he arrives in town.'

There was dead silence.

'Where's he been bitten?' I asked.

The dead silence continued.

'Joe, are you there?' I said. 'Where's Roota been bitten?'

'Look, Doc, I can't speak too loud 'cause I'm ringing from the pub. There's a few of the blokes here and all they know is that Roota's been bit b' a snake, but I haven't told them exactly where.'

'But I've got to know exactly where he's been bitten, Joe,' I said, avoiding the question as to what he was doing in the pub with 'a few of the blokes' at that hour of the morning. 'Joe, can you hear me?'

'On the penis,' came the whisper.

Well, that certainly got me thinking. I mean, Roota's Roota and the many and varied stories of his sexual exploits were known far and wide, but how in the hell a bloke could've got himself bitten in that spot defied imagination.

'On the what?' I asked.

'You heard me. Roota's been bit on the penis,' came the answer, fractionally louder.

Well, that was clear enough. It also explained Big Joe's apprehension about having to give first aid. You could just imagine the comments from the blokes in the pub as they watched Joe apply pressure immobilisation to Roota Kozlowski, especially with it being in that particular region. And so soon after the magazine article and all. Joe'd never live it down.

'Look, Joe,' I said, 'I know what's going through your mind, mate, but you've got to forget all that rubbish. The point is, if you don't give the treatment, Roota could well die. Do I make myself very clear, Joe?'

Silence.

'So, Joe,' I continued, 'as soon as Roota arrives, get him to whip down his pants, then apply pressure immobilisation. And what's more, hold onto it until I get there, right.'

Silence.

'Do you hear me, Joe!'

'Okay,' came the reluctant reply.

As the story goes, Roota pulled into town not too much later, very groggy from the snake bite. He blundered into the pub and saw Joe over by the bar with a few of the blokes, all of them looking extremely downcast.

'Have yer spoken to the doctor?' Roota asked.

'Yes,' Joe mumbled.

'What did he say?'

'Well, Roota,' Joe said, 'doc reckons yer gonna die.'

The Pie-Eyed Piper

(Swampy)

There was trouble in the district. Foxes were taking chooks at a *disasterous* rate. Fresh eggs were as scarce as hens' teeth. Or even hens for that matter. Only the corrugated-iron and chicken-wire fortress of Mrs Brown's chooks run had remained untouched. So when the foxes started breaking in there, drastic measures had to be taken.

When all local efforts had met with failure, the townspeople got together and formed a fox watch committee to rid us of this verminous problem.

An advertisement was placed in all local, city and interstate newspapers in an attempt to attract professional fox hunters to the district. A reward of £100 was offered to the most successful hunter, plus free beer, food and lodgings at the pub for the duration of their stay.

Well, these fox hunters came from far and near, armed with all sorts of contraptions and ideas, only to end up walking away with their tails between their legs, foxless ... and Mrs Brown's precious chooks still on the decline.

Now along with the many genuine fox hunters came the freeloaders, seemingly more interested in the offer of 'free beer, food and lodgings' than any attempt to catch cunning foxes. A couple in particular stood out. Their names were Goodtime Charlie and Brewery Bob. They arrived soon after the advertisement's placement and hadn't moved from the bar stools they first occupied.

The fox watch committee met and decided to tell these two blokes to move along. But Goodtime Charlie explained to all that they were just waiting for the rush of hunters to subside before their master plan was put into action.

'We will catch all the foxes in the district on the third evening from this day,' slurred Goodtime Charlie.

That bit of news even caught Brewery Bob off guard and he almost fell from his bar stool with shock.

'Blimey, Charlie, not that soon, surely!' he exclaimed.

But Goodtime Charlie remained liquidly adamant. All the locals were told to report to the pub armed to the teeth and ready to catch foxes in three evenings' time.

Goodtime Charlie then held a secret meeting (even minus Brewery Bob) with Mrs Brown who, other than being the owner of disappearing chooks, happened to be the CWA's sewing committee president.

On the third evening the locals arrived at the pub as agreed, only to find Goodtime Charlie drinking alone. Upon asking of Brewery Bob's whereabouts, we were told that he'd gone to Mrs Brown's place to try on a new suit. It was a pleasant enough evening so everyone sat outside the pub, awaiting Goodtime Charlie's orders.

Then, in the distance, someone saw a small cloud of dust from over Mrs Brown's way. Everyone gathered to watch as it headed towards town, slowly growing larger. Then from out of the middle of the dust cloud appeared the largest chook you could imagine. About six foxes were in hot pursuit. They must've thought all their Christmases had come at once. Over the rise and down toward the creek came that monster chook … assorted animals joining in the chase.

'It's Brewery Bob in a chook suit with flippers on!' shouted Bluey Saunders, the barman.

Out of the creek flew Brewery Bob, chased by a dozen or so

foxes, four dingoes, three feral cats and an emu. Down into the main street — it looked like a stampede.

'I'll kill you, Charlie!' came the cry from out of the dust cloud. Stepping back into the pub, everyone took up battle positions.

Brewery Bob burst through the front bar door, taking it clean off its hinges. The collected menagerie followed.

After the dust had settled and all captured animals counted, the final tally came to sixteen foxes, eight dingoes, seven feral cats, three emus, two kangaroos, two goannas, a couple of galahs, a pet poodle and a budgerigar.

Brewery Bob began to lose some of his anger as he was showered in adulation. But he refused point blank to talk to Goodtime Charlie. Their partnership had sadly come to its end.

The following morning, Brewery Bob took his half of the £100 reward and headed off to the big smoke to 'find a woman and settle down'.

Goodtime Charlie decided to settle down too, in his own sort of way. As undisputed chief fox hunter, he declared he'd accept Beckom's kind offer of 'free beer, food and lodgings'.

Goodtime Charlie became a permanent resident of the pub.

There's a Redback on the ...

(Great Australian Outback School Stories)

Yes, well my name's Anne. I'm currently living in the Brisbane area but, back in the early 1970s, I went over to the Northern Territory where I took up a position as a schoolteacher on Brunette Downs Station. A very young and naive teacher too, I may add. Now to give you some idea, Brunette Downs is in the Barkly Tablelands area, about four hundred and fifty kilometres north-west of Mount Isa. At that stage it also happened to be one of the biggest cattle stations in Australia, being something like just over twelve thousand square miles. So it's pretty big.

I'm not sure just who runs Brunette Downs these days but back then it was owned by King Ranch Australia and while I was there it was my job to teach all the Aboriginal kids on the property. And I can tell you, being more or less a city girl, I had to very rapidly learn as much as I could about the Aboriginal people, their ways and their culture. And they certainly don't teach you that sort of stuff at teachers' college. So I went through a very steep learning curve. Almost perpendicular. But once I'd settled into it I really enjoyed the experience and I learnt a lot during my time out there and, to this day, I really believe that we, as white people, could learn a hell of a lot from the Aboriginal people; for instance, as far as caring for family goes.

Anyhow, all that aside, there I was on Brunette Downs and one day I was teaching these kids in the school room when I felt this thing crawling on my neck. Must be a fly, I thought, so I tried to wave it away, you know, like you do. But it just wouldn't budge. So I gave it a slap and as I squashed it, it felt just like someone had placed some burning tongs on my neck. This's not good, I thought, and when I took a look at what I'd squashed, I realised I'd been bitten by a redback spider.

By then it was almost lunchtime so I said to the kids, 'Look, how about you go out for lunch a bit early today,' and when they'd gone I went up to the clinic to see the nursing sister up there. A funny sort of person she was, too, I might add.

'I've just been bitten on the neck by a redback spider,' I said.

'Oh,' she said, and she gave me a vacant sort of look. 'Are they poisonous?'

'Yes, of course they are,' I said, astounded that she didn't seem to know the first thing about spider bites.

'Oh,' she replied, 'then I'd better get in touch with the Flying Doctor to see what we can do about it.'

'Thanks for all your help,' I replied, with just a little more than a hint of sarcasm.

So while she was trying to get in touch with the Royal Flying Doctor Service I went to my room where I had a first-aid book from teachers' college — an ancient old thing it was — and I had a look in that. It said that if you're bitten by a spider, the first thing you should do is to put a tourniquet on. Well that seemed a bit ridiculous, especially with me having been bitten on the neck. Anyhow, by that time I was feeling quite sick. I was also starting to get quite a fever so I decided to go to bed which, as it turned out, was the best thing for me to do.

In the meantime the nurse had been on the radio to the Royal Flying Doctor Service and explained my situation to the doctor. Apparently she was told to treat the situation just like I was in shock and to keep a close watch for any further developments.

Now, what you've got to realise here is that, out there, when anyone's talking over the radio to the RFDS or to School of the Air or whoever, every Tom, Dick and Mary within cooee is able to listen in on the conversation. And mind you, they do, and all the time. So unbeknown to me, my being bitten on the neck by this wretched redback spider ended up being broadcast throughout the Northern Territory and over into western Queensland.

Anyhow I survived.

Then a couple of months later a few of us went to this picnic race meeting up at Borroloola, which is up on the Gulf of Carpentaria, on the McArthur River. That was quite an extraordinary place, too. And oh dear, didn't we have a time and a half up there. It was an absolute hoot. I tell you, my life-education kept expanding non-stop and at a rapid rate while I was teaching in the Territory.

Anyhow, there I was at Borroloola and I ran into this guy from Mallapunyah Station. Mallapunyah is something like three hundred and fifty kilometres north-west of Tennant Creek. And, well, this bloke was a sort of a legend around the area. So anyhow he came up to me and he said, 'Oh, gee,' he said, in his real droll, laconic bush voice, 'so you're the teacher from Brunette Downs, are yer? The one what got bit on the neck by the redback spider.'

'Yes,' I said, 'that was me. Why?'

And he just stood there for I don't know how long, ogling at me; you know, eyeing me up and down from tip to toe. Quite embarrassing it was really. Then after he'd had a good hard look he shook his head from side to side and he said, 'Jeez,' he said. 'I would'a liked to 'a been that redback spider.'

The Docking of Springy Wilkenson

(Great Australian Shearing Stories)

Now this isn't exactly a shearing story but it did take place in a shearing shed, dead set. I know. Anyway, one day the Whittaker kids arrived at the Wilkensons' sheep property and asked their schoolmate Springy if he wouldn't mind showing them through the shearing shed. It was for a school project or something, they said. Now, Springy Wilkenson was certainly no great shakes at school. He wasn't one of your higher intellectuals, as he himself would testify, but at the ripe old age of eleven he most certainly considered himself to be a man of vast wisdom and experience where sheep and shearing were concerned.

'Yeah, okay, I'll show yer about,' said Springy, and he spat in the direction of nowhere. 'Folla me,' he added and off he went through the penning-up yards and into the shearing shed with the Whittakers hot on his heels.

Now the Whittakers were a motley bunch, comprised of a smattering of both boys and girls of ten and under. But, for kids that age, it struck Springy that they certainly had inquisitive minds.

'Whata they do with that thing, Springy?' one asked.

'She's a wool press, young feller,' answered Springy, then he went on to explain, almost correctly, its workings. 'Did some pressin' meself last season,' he added, which seemed to impress the Whittaker kids no end, especially the girls.

'Wow,' they gasped.

'What 'appens 'ere, on this 'ere table-lookin' thing?' asked another of the Whittakers.

'Well,' replied Springy, 'that's where they class the wool, you know; give it a grade 'n stuff. Sort the good from the bad, like. Did a bit meself last season,' he added for maximum effect.

'Wow,' said the Whittaker kids.

And so the guided tour continued through the shearing shed and down along the stands. 'What's this, Springy?' 'What's that, Springy?' And Springy came up with answers to all their questions, even answers to the questions he didn't have a clue about. But, still, the Whittaker kids were obviously impressed by his knowledge and even more so by his manner and experience.

'Did a bit meself last season,' he'd add, almost casually.

'Wow,' they'd reply.

Anyway, down past the stands there was a small room, just off to the side a bit. That's where Springy's dad kept his assorted array of accumulated sheep farming and shearing tools, odds and sods and bits and pieces.

'What's that thing, Springy?' asked one of the Whittaker girls after they'd entered.

'She's what's called a paira docking pliers and yer use 'em fer takin' the tails offa the lambs,' answered Springy. 'Did a bit meself last season, I did. You know, docked a few, like.'

'How's it work then?' the girl asked.

So Springy took down the docking pliers and gave it to the Whittakers so that they could have a closer gander. Then, after they'd finished, Springy launched into an explanation about how the apparatus worked. He said that it was similar to a normal pair of pliers, but in reverse, inasmuch as when you squeezed the handle end, the four prongs at the other end opened out, not closed, as with normal pliers.

But even after Springy's lengthy explanation, the Whittaker kids, well, they still couldn't quite come to grips with its workings. So, to demonstrate, Springy took a rubber ring, an elastrator, out of its box and placed it around the four prongs of the docking pliers. Then, when he squeezed the handle of the pliers, the four prongs spread apart and, in doing so, stretched the rubber ring.

'Wow,' gasped one of the Whittakers. 'What 'appens then?'

'Well,' explained Springy, 'yer slip her over the taila the lamb 'n then the tail falls off.'

Now you could see from the faces of the Whittakers that they were beginning to understand the actual mechanics of the docking pliers but, as to how the tail of the lamb came to fall off, posed another question.

'Why's the tail fall off, Springy?'

'Well young feller, the rubba ring cuts off the blood circularisation in the lamb's tail, see, causin' the tail ta fall offa the lamb.'

'Whatd'yer mean, circularisation?' asked one of the Whittakers.

'Look,' said Springy, 'I'll show yer how she works.' And Springy started looking around for something that would simulate a lamb's tail.

'What'a yer lookin' fer?' asked one of the Whittakers.

'I'm lookin' fer somethin' like a lamb's tail or somethin' so as I can show yers how she works,' Springy replied.

'What about usin' yer dick?' giggled one of the more world-wise and imaginative Whittaker girls.

'Yeah, I was thinkin' that meself,' said Springy, not wanting to be outdone in the ideas department, especially by a girl.

So Springy undid his flies and pulled out his penis. 'Wow,' came a gasp from the Whittaker kids, the girls in particular.

'Now,' said Springy, 'here's how she works.' Then he placed one of the rubber rings around the top of the four prongs of the pliers. 'So yer open her up just like that,' Springy continued, as he opened up the pliers. 'Then yer slip her over the lamb's tail ... just like that ...'

'N' how's the rubba ring get from offa the pliers 'n onta the tail?' asked one of the Whittakers.

'Well,' said Springy, 'yer just let her go. There, see ... just like that.'

Now, it took a split second before it dawned upon Springy that he'd allowed the rubber ring to slide off the docking pliers and onto the butt of his penis.

'N' how yer gonna get the rubba ring off, Springy?' asked one of the Whittakers.

But by then Springy had run out of answers. Completely. He even opened his mouth in the vague hope that some words might miraculously pop out and save him. But they didn't. So he just stood there with his mouth agape and stared at his penis as it turned from red to blue, then from blue to purple. And it was somewhere during this eclipse of colour that Springy realised he was in big trouble. Big, big trouble, indeed.

'How long's it gonna take fer yer dick ta fall off, Springy?' asked one of the Whittaker kids.

Panic hit Springy like a sledge hammer. His mind started working at such a rapid pace that you could just about hear the cogs spinning around in his head. The only trouble was that they were spinning in neutral. Then suddenly they crunched into gear as he was hit by an idea. There was only one person who could save him.

'Mum!' Springy shouted and he took off back through the shearing shed, out the door, and across toward his house, screaming, 'Mum! Mum! One of them Whittaker kids's gone 'n docked me!'

Now, the instant Springy's mum saw her son's 'pre-dick-ament', she quickly dragged him into the bathroom and that's the last the Whittakers saw of Springy, for a whole month.

And that's a fair dinkum story and, do you know how I know? Well, I'll give you a hint. I walk with a spring in my step, always have. So I'll leave the rest up to you!

The Tooth Fairy

(The Complete Book of Australian Flying Doctor Stories)

This is one of Fred McKay's stories. It isn't mine so you'll have to check the details with him.

It happened back in the late 1930s, long before John Flynn died and Fred took over. Fred and Meg had recently been married and they were visiting a cattle station out in the Barkly Tablelands, just over the Queensland border, into the Northern Territory. Anyway, the station's storekeeper-cum-bookkeeper had an abscessed molar, very painful it was.

'Meg'll sort it out,' Fred offered, brimming with confidence in his new wife.

Now, even though she'd completed a two-week crash course in 'tooth extraction' at the Brisbane Dental Hospital before they'd set out, Meg didn't quite share Fred's enthusiasm in her ability. She was new to this rugged bush lifestyle. As you might imagine, it was a big change for someone who was virtually a city girl and she was still trying to find her feet among the dust, the flies, the heat, the cold, the camping out, the cattle, the bore water, the stockmen. Still, she tentatively agreed to give it a go.

But whatever minimal confidence she had completely vanished when Meg arrived at the store. The storekeeper looked a formidable customer indeed. He was a huge man, a mountain in comparison to the 'dental-dummy' that Meg had trained on back in Brisbane. To make matters worse, when the news had spread that a woman was going to have a go at extracting the storekeeper's molar, a crowd of sceptical stockman had gathered, all eager to watch the event unfold.

Until that point in time, Meg had hardly ever pulled a tooth, let alone done it in front of a crowd as rough and as doubting as this mob was. Still, she couldn't turn back now. She'd volunteered her services and she'd have to see it through to the end, whatever that end may be. So she sat the chap down on an old box outside the station store. She gave him an injection and then set to with the pliers or whatever.

Now you might be able to imagine some of the remarks coming from the stockmen when it became obvious that the harder Meg pulled on the molar, the more it seemed that it wasn't going to budge. And the more the molar wouldn't budge, the more anxious the storekeeper became about allowing a woman to attempt to extract his tooth. But if there was one golden rule that Meg had learned in at the Brisbane Dental Hospital, it was 'Once you've got a good grip, never let go.'

So she didn't.

She latched onto that molar and she pulled with every ounce of strength she could muster. Even when the storekeeper started to gargle a protest, Meg straddled him and still hung on and pulled. And when he struggled to free himself from off the old box, Meg clambered up on the box and still hung on and pulled. Then, as the storekeeper attempted to walk away, Meg gave an almighty twist and yank and ... out came the tooth.

Well, this brought the house down, so to speak. As Meg stood there in complete triumph displaying the molar, the gathering of stockmen exploded into cheers, whistles and applause. But the person that was most stunned was the beefy storekeeper himself. He gazed down upon Meg in complete wonderment and, with the tears pouring down his cheeks and the blood running down his chin, he called out, 'What a woman!'

Dead Drunk

(Great Australian Railway Stories)

I'm eighty-six in October and it's twenty-one years since I retired from the railways. What happened was that, during the war, I was in New Guinea and Borneo and, when that finished, I come to Parkes and someone said they were looking for cleaners up at the loco depot. Cleaning's like, you black-oil the steam engines then rub it in with cotton waste. It's like polishing your boots, which was something I'd done a heck of a lot of during the war. So I was cleaning for a while, then they sent me down to Sydney for an exam. That's how I passed the acting fireman's job.

Then from acting fireman I went to a fireman. Then I went for an acting driver and finally, I passed for driver. We used to run to Orange, to Cootamundra, freight to Dubbo, then we'd run out through Euabalong West, where we'd camp in the barracks, before going on to Ivanhoe the next day.

But there was a railways chap I remember; they called him 'Eggy' because his name was Eggleston, and this Eggy was a real drinker. My God, he could drink. And probably because nobody could put up with him and his drinking, that's why he remained single. Anyhow, Eggy lived in a room out there in the railway barracks and he had this big black dog he called 'Smart Dog'. So Eggy came home this night as full as a boot and he found the dog sleeping in his bed, so he said, 'Come on, Smart Dog, get off.'

And Smart Dog started growling at him, so Eggy said, 'Yer worse than a bloody wife you are, Smart Dog.' And he grabbed a blanket and he went and slept on the couch while his dog stayed in his bed. Then another time he drank so much that he poisoned himself with the alcohol. He was that bad that he was comatose and he needed to see a doctor. So they put him on one of those trolley things that the porters used to carry all the luggage around on. Anyhow, they wheeled him out of the barracks and up onto the railway platform and, because he was still out to it, they just threw a sheet over him and left him lying there, on this trolley, while they went to get the doctor.

Anyhow, it just so happened that while they were away, two old women came walking along the platform and they saw this porter's trolley, and they could see that under the sheet was this human body. Anyway, one old woman said to the other, 'Oh, it's such a terrible thing to leave a corpse just laying out on the platform like that.'

'Yes,' said the other, 'God rest this poor lost soul.'

Then they both started to cross themselves and mutter their silent prayers to departed spirits or whatever, and while they were muttering away and crossing themselves Eggy suddenly let out a pitiful groan from under the sheet.

Well, you should've seen those two old ducks. They thought they'd raised the dead.

Shagger's Ears

(Great Australian Shearing Stories)

When I left high school, my father had an apprenticeship all lined up for me as a carpenter but, no, I went straight on the shit stick instead. That's what they call it when you're shearing, the 'shit stick'.

So I was about seventeen or eighteen when I officially started. But there were no real guns around here back then, you know, two-hundred-a-day-men. And of course, naturally, you picked up some pretty bad habits because there was nobody to show you the right way to go about things. You just followed the other fellers. That's how you learnt. That's how it was done. Then a bloke by the name of George Mooney came into our team. George hailed from around here, around the south-west of New South Wales, but he'd shore up in Queensland and all. And George took me aside.

'See those two fellers up here,' he said. There were six of us in the team. 'Well they've been shearing for a long time and they've never shore a hundred. And, what's more, by the way they're going about it they're never likely to, neither.'

So George got me going and I sort of copied his style, his technique, so to speak. See, imagine you're long-blowing a sheep and you're holding it all wrong. For instance, I used to stretch its front leg out and lay him flat on his back. But after about three or four blows he'd start to kick and George'd say, 'Let his leg go.' Then he'd show me. He'd hold the leg for the first two blows then he'd let it go and it helped the sheep relax. It helped the sheep to relax, see. And I've never forgotten that. That's the first thing I think of, all these years later.

But I tell you, I've bumped into some funny men, shearers like, over the years. I remember we had one bloke come down from Rockhampton — 'The Owl', we called him. And, mind you, he looked like a fucking owl, too: big round eyes, the works. Anyway, other than looking like an owl he also acted like one. He'd come in and go, 'ooh, ooh'. He'd hoot, just like an owl. Always hooting like an owl, he was. That's how he'd greet you.

But the Owl was all there, though. He was okay, like, intelligent and all. And he could fucking shear. There was no doubting that. But he just kept carrying on with all this owl shit. Like one day we were out at this place, a four-stander it was, and the Owl went back into his catching pen. Then, when he didn't come back, I looked around and there he was squatting up on the big oregon board, prancing around like an owl. 'Ooh, ooh,' he goes. 'I'm the Owl. I sent a roustabout mad once. Ooh, ooh.'

And I didn't doubt that he would've, neither. Anyhow, this time Hank Foster was there, roust-abouting he was, and Hank'd had enough.

'I'll give him fucking owl, alright,' Hank reckoned. So, while the Owl's shearing away, Hank climbs up on the top railing, about seven or eight bloody feet off the floor, directly above the Owl. Of course, the Owl's in deep concentration so he doesn't notice a thing. Then, all of a sudden, Hank lets out this almighty scream, 'Ooh! Ooh!' Just like a fucking owl. Then he jumps right down, right beside the Owl. It frightened the shit out of him, it did.

The only trouble was that it all sort of backfired a bit because when Hank hit the floor, one of his legs went clean through the fucking floorboards. So there's the Owl, hooting away with his eyes just about popping out of his head with the shock of it all. And there's Hank, stuck in the floor, looking up at him, making strange squeaky-owl noises.

So that was the Owl.

Then there's a different story, and this one's all about how shearers can have a lend of you. I was working with Kenny Parslow, who was the shearing contractor by that stage. Anyway, in the team there was this chap called Victor. Now, this Victor was a pretty shy and retiring sort of character. Very timid he was, and he'd recently got back from his honeymoon.

'Jeez, Victor,' one of the roustabouts said, pretending to act all concerned. 'Yer've lost a hell of a lota weight since yer was married, mate.'

'Have I?' Victor replied, taking the bait.

'Yeah. I'd reckon it's from all that shagging yer done while yer was on yer honeymoon,' the roustie added.

'Well, I don't know about that,' said Victor, who was by now looking decidedly embarrassed.

'Oh, well then,' the roustabout said, 'I'll soon tell yer.' So he got Victor to turn around and, when he had, the roustabout took a close look behind Victor's ears. 'Well, there yer go,' the roustie announced after his examination. 'It's obvious that yer done a bloody lot of heavy shagging, just of late.'

Then somebody said, 'Well why's that?'

'Well if yer come and have a look here, behind Victor's ear,' he said, 'you'll see that he's gone all white, and that's what happens when you do a lot of heavy shagging.'

So all the shearers gathered around and they took a look behind Victor's ears.

'Jeez, yer bloody right,' they chorused.

'It's a bloody wonder that yer didn't come back from yer honeymoon all skin 'n bone, Victor,' said the roustie, and the rest of the blokes grunted and groaned their agreement.

But the thing was, see, these blokes was only having Victor on. They were only having a lend of him, like, because you don't go white behind the ears from heavy shagging, do you? But Victor wasn't aware of that. He didn't know. I mean, he was the type of bloke that could well have even been a virgin before he got married. He more than likely was.

So, any rate, when I went outside at lunchtime to have a wash, there's this Victor, standing in front of the mirror, screwing his fucking head around at all angles in an attempt to get a look behind his ears. All contorting himself he was, I can tell you.

But I mean, you meet fellers like that, lots of them. Blokes like Blowfly Brown, Billy Cassidy, Lorrie Spencer, Johnny White, Hank Foster, like I mentioned, and then there's Dick Knowles, he's one of the funniest men I've ever known. But they're all good blokes. Well, most of them are, anyway.

So no, I went straight into shearing after high school and I enjoyed it, so I stuck with it. And it's been pretty good to me. I've reared a family of six. I shore for near on twenty years and I still do a few. Quite a few of the fellers around my age are still at it. Take John Stout, from down at Ardlethan, for instance. He's sixty in September and he's been shearing ever since he left high school. And he's still a shearing contractor and a bloody good one too. So that's not a bad stint, neither, is it, eh? Not bad at all.

But no, you get some funny sorts of fellers out in the sheds.

Getting the Job Done

(Great Australian Outback Trucking Stories)

I'd been an owner-driver for near on forty years and, over that time, my business had grown into quite a success. The thing is, to make any sort of a go of it in the trucking industry, you've got to be prepared to work seven days a week, twelve months of the year — no exceptions. And that meant I was hardly ever home. So my marriage suffered and we eventually split up. Still, driving was pretty much all I knew, so I kept at it right up until I faced some quite serious health issues. By then I was near on seventy and, like, my knees were giving me hell, my hip was playing up something terrible and the doctors told me that my heart wasn't ticking along as well as it should. And that's when I made the decision to call it quits and take things a bit more easy. So I sold the whole show, lock stock and barrel, and at a pretty good price too I might add.

But after I'd sold the business, I just couldn't seem to settle down. Trucks had virtually been my entire life and so I was soon pretty antsy and, I guess you could say, I kind of lost my way a bit. Sitting around doing nothing wasn't for me. Then out of the blue the supervisor from the local council got in touch. He'd heard that I was at a bit of a loose end and he wanted to know if I'd like to fill in for one of their workers who'd gone off on stress leave. The first job I got involved in was driving the pothole truck. That's the truck that goes out with all the gear and gravel and tar to fill in the potholes in the road. Anyhow, I jumped at the chance. It'd not only get me out of the house, but I'd also be back in the cab of a truck, driving once more. You beauty.

'Great,' I said. 'When do you want me to start?'

'Tomorrow,' he said. The he added, as a word of warning, 'We run a pretty tight ship here.'

'That's fine by me,' I said.

'Good,' and then he went on to detail what my strict daily schedule was to be. I was to report at the council depot at 7 a.m. sharp where I'd meet up with two fellers — the 'potholers'. The supervisor would then brief the three of us as to where we were to go that day. The truck would already be loaded with everything that was needed to fill in the potholes, including any leftover gravel and tar from the previous day's work. At 7.30 a.m. I was to drive the two potholers out of the council depot and head off to our destination. Upon our arrival we'd work till morning tea time, which was to begin at 9.30 a.m. and finish at 9.45 a.m. After our morning tea break we'd get back to it and we'd work right up till midday, which was lunchtime. Lunch break was three-quarters of an hour. Then it was back to work again and, depending on how far we were from the depot, we'd have to pack up our gear and get back by 4 o'clock. We were then allowed half an hour to clean up and so forth, before we knocked off at 4.30 p.m.

So that was the plan.

On the first morning I arrived at 7 a.m. sharp. The supervisor was there but the two potholers were yet to turn up. So, with what looked like a bit of time up my sleeve, I asked the supervisor if I could go off and buy a newspaper. That was all okay and I arrived back just as the potholers rolled in at just after 7.30. One was fat and tall and middle-aged and the other one was small and skinny and middle-aged, and neither of them looked too good. The term 'as crook as a dog' comes to mind. Though in this case they looked like two very crook dogs. Anyhow, they then apologised to the supervisor for being late. From what I could gather, one of them had had a birthday party the night before, things had got out of hand, the alarm hadn't gone off and so they'd slept in.

The supervisor seemed none too pleased about their excuse, but not wanting to upset the strict daily schedule any further than it already had been, he forged ahead and read out our instructions. We were to begin the day's potholing at a spot about forty-five kilometres out of town. The potholers didn't seem to have the faintest clue as to where we had to go — either that or, because of their condition, they wouldn't have cared where they ended up. It was just lucky that I'd grown up in the area and I knew the exact spot the supervisor had mentioned. Anyhow, by the time the two potholers had dressed into their overalls and work boots and had put on their safety vests and had crawled into the truck, it'd gone 8.15.

It must've been one hell of a birthday party because, not long after I'd driven out the front gate of the depot, they'd both fallen asleep. But that didn't worry me. Having been an owner-driver, I was used to being in a truck by myself. And anyway, it was good to be back in the cab again. So I'm just driving along, enjoying my own company, when one of the potholers wakes from his slumber and says, 'How long before we get there?'

'About another fifteen minutes,' I say.

He takes a look at his watch, and says, 'Gee, mate, yer rushin' it.' He said, 'Slow it down a bit. We don't have ter be there till mornin' tea time.'

'Oh, okay.'

So I slowed down to pretty much a crawl and he falls back to sleep. Meanwhile his mate's still snoring away.

Anyhow, we arrive at the spot just before morning tea time, 9.30. So it's out of the truck and out with the Thermos and they wash down a few Panadol with piping hot tea. But now there's another hiccup. They now declared that they were unable to start work until the Panadol kicked in. So morning tea goes overtime and it's not till 10 o'clock that it looks like we might get some work done. It's my job to keep the truck moving along in slow motion while these two fellers follow along behind, filling in each of the potholes with gravel and tar, then tamping it down.

Now, being a bloke who's usually always on the go, it's not long before I get bored.

'Hey fellers,' I say, 'do you want a hand?'

'No, mate,' comes the reply. 'It's your job ter drive the truck 'n it's our job ter fill in the potholes.'

You know, perhaps there's some sort of specialised course in potholing that you have to pass. And that gets me thinking, if there was, by the looks of it, one of the main subjects must've been 'the art of leaning on a shovel without breaking the handle'. Anyhow, it wasn't my job to kick up a stink. I was only there till the other feller came back from stress leave. So I don't say anything. I just stayed in the truck and I got back to rereading the newspaper.

But the thing was — see, around this area, everybody knows everybody. And the last thing I wanted was for someone to drive past and see that I was sitting in the truck doing bugger all. Like, I'd be labelled a slack-arse, and I didn't want to get landed with that sort of reputation. So whenever a car came down the road, I'd duck down and hide behind the newspaper till they'd passed.

Anyhow, we inched along the road till it was lunchtime. Lunch break was extended by half an hour due to the potholers having to take some extra time off till the Panadol for their ongoing and continuing hangovers kicked in. So it wasn't till around 1.15 that they meandered back to work. By 3 o'clock I'd read the newspaper about four times, from front to back and then back again and we'd covered a kilometre of road and filled in five potholes. And that's when they decided to call it quits. Their previous night's activities had finally got the better of them.

'That's enough for the day,' they announced and they tossed their shovels and whatnot onto the truck and they crawled back up into the cab with me.

I said, 'Don't you reckon it's a bit too early for us to get back to the depot?'

'You're right,' they replied. 'We'll hang around here for another half an hour and then you can drive us back.'

'Oh, okay,' I said and they both went back to sleep while I continued to pretend to reread the newspaper.

Anyhow, I eventually got them back to the council depot at 3.45, which was a little bit earlier than was scheduled. As it happened, the lady in the office told us that the supervisor had gone off to some sort of business meeting — my immediate thought was, probably down the pub — and so the two potholers disappeared into the lunch room and played darts till it was knock-off time.

Now, I don't know just how many birthdays two blokes of around the same age can fit into the one month, but these two potholers seemed to celebrate one of their birthdays just about every bloody night of the week. Which got me thinking that, perhaps, they were sponsored by Panadol; I don't know. And the snail's pace that they worked at was nothing short of embarrassing. Adding to all that, one of the potholers turned out to be quite an odd sort of bloke. He was the short skinny one. Now, with all this political correctness crap, I don't know if you're allowed to use such a term anymore, but I'd describe him as being a touch 'backward'. Maybe it was because of his many years of alcohol consumption, I don't know, but he had a vacant stare about him and his speech wasn't quite right.

Anyhow, a couple of days later, after we get out there, he said, 'Let's have lunch at the Soft Wok.'

'Great idea,' said his mate.

Now, as I might've said, I'd grown up in this area, but, for the life of me, I'd never heard of a place that went by the name of the Soft Wok. So I said, 'Where the hell's the Soft Wok?'

'Down by the river,' he says.

'Really?' I said.

'Yep,' was the reply.

Anyway, I let it be and went back to my newspaper reading. Then, when it got to lunchtime, they downed tools and they got back into the truck and I was given directions as to where the Soft Wok was. And that's when I discovered that the 'Soft Wok' wasn't an Asian restaurant as I'd imagined; it was actually quite a large rock, down by the river, which was covered in moss. So that's where we went to eat lunch. And when that was done, and they'd taken their dose of Panadol, they stretched out on the moss and went to sleep. So that was their Soft Wok. And while we were working out that way, we visited the Soft Wok quite often. And, depending on how hungover they were, that's where they'd stay till I could talk them into going back to work.

Anyhow, after a week or so of this sort of palaver, the supervisor got me into his office and he said, 'Listen, John, the blokes reckon you're pushing them a bit too hard, so I might put you on another job.'

I said, 'Mate, I was just trying to get the job done.'

'Doesn't matter,' he said. 'We've already got one bloke out on stress leave. The last thing we need is for two more to follow him.' He said, 'And anyway, I've got a more suitable job for you.'

Now this was when they were putting in a new bypass. Anyway, for whatever reason, the council had put in for the subcontracting job of carting around all the road-making gear. And the supervisor had been right. It was more to my liking. At least I was driving a fair-dinkum truck. I forget just now but it was either a 400 or a 404 Kenworth.

Anyhow, this particular day I only had a single trailer because I was taking a road compactor up to the work site. So I drive up there. It might've been a Sunday; I can't remember. But I'm just about to unload the road compactor when this feller comes running across.

'Hey, mate,' he says, 'you can't unload it today.'

I said, 'Why not?'

He said, 'Well, over on the pad where you're supposed to unload the compactor there's two snakes mating.'

I said, 'Yes, so what?'

He said, 'Well, the snake catcher won't be in till tomorr'a and it's his job to catch the snakes and relocate them.'

Fair dinkum. That's what he said; as true as I stand here. They had a special snake catcher, employed on the site, to catch and remove snakes.

I thought, Well, bugger this. So I grabbed a shovel out of the truck and I walked over to these two mating snakes and *whack, whack* I killed them both, just like that.

The feller said, 'Hey, mate, you can't do that. We're supposed to relocate them.'

I said, 'Don't worry. I'll relocate them allright.' I said, 'As soon as I unload the compactor, I'll chuck the bastards onto my trailer and I'll drop 'em off when I get down the road a bit.'

Which I did, and a day or so later the supervisor called me into his office and he ticked me off for my — and I quote — 'disregard of environmental awareness'.

I said, 'Mate, I was just trying to get the job done.'

'Doesn't matter,' he said. 'Rules are rules, and anyway, the bloke who was out on stress leave looks like he might be coming back to work next week.'

So that was it. Within that one month, I'd not only been accused of pushing the two potholers too hard, but I was also being branded as a snake murderer. And so that was the end of my very short career working as a truck driver with the council.

Big Ned from Big Burrawong

(Great Australian Shearing Stories)

I got a real ball-tearer here for you, mate. Now, I don't know if anyone else has told you the one about the shearer, Big Ned Barrett from Big Burrawong Station or not but, if they have, forget it, because it's a complete and utter load of bull. But if you've got a minute to spare I'll more than gladly relate to you the real, true, fair-dinkum, ridgy-didge, authentic story, which was told to me by an old shearer known to all, simply, as Old Jack.

Now Old Jack was the most honest shearer you could ever meet; so honest in fact that it's often been stated that an untruth had never passed through his own teeth. That's why I've got no doubt at all as to the authenticity of the story, even though, unfortunately, on the day that he told it to me Old Jack had misplaced his own false teeth and was wearing his late wife's spare set.

So, in keeping with the truthful nature of the story, I've written it down word for word, which I'll now relate to you.

As Old Jack tells it, a good while ago he was shearing in the largest shed in Australia, if not the world. This shed was known as Big Burrawong. Now just to give you some idea, on Big Burrawong Station they had so many sheep that they shore all year round. It was something like painting the Sydney Harbour Bridge. There could've been millions of sheep. No one knew, not even Old Jack, and he wasn't sure because he said that every time he attempted to count the sheep on the property, he'd fall asleep well before he even got out of the second-reserve penning-up yard. But with having so many sheep to shear, the owners had to employ thousands of shearers, plus hundreds of roustabouts, pressers and such. Then to feed all of these workers they had to employ a great number of cooks; so many in fact that they employed cooks to cook for the cooks. So that's how big the place was.

Now to give you some idea of the logistics of catering for such a large number of people, the amount of food consumed was measured in hundreds of tons per day. And, what's more, the actual billy that they boiled the water up in was a specially manufactured tank which was so deep and wide that the cooks had to launch a rowing boat so they could go out on the boiling water to mix in the tea for smoko.

Big Burrawong was that big. Not a word of a lie.

Anyway, as Old Jack told me, at this shed there was a shearer working there who went by the name of Big Ned Barrett. Now this Big Ned was a massive feller, massive he was. But not only that, Big Ned was also touted as being Australia's top shearer at that time. Old Jack reckoned him to be a good deal faster than the well-known Jackie Howe and twice as fast as Jackie's slightly less well known twin brothers, Any and Some Howe. But as history won't tell you, Big Ned's exploits on the board were never recorded. And that's mainly because the shearing contractor at Big Burrawong, a bloke known to the taxation department as Shifty Sam, thought that those people who'd never seen Big Ned shear might've thought his truly recorded exploits to be a complete fabrication.

Big Ned was that good. Not a word of a lie.

Now one day, during a spell of wet weather when they couldn't shear, Big Ned decided to go out in the boat with the cooks to see how many shovelfuls of tea they put into the boiling water. But, unfortunately, by the time they got near the epicentre of this gigantic billy, the boiling water became so turbulent that it caused Big Ned to get seasick. And while he was being seasick, he fell out of the boat and *'splash!'* into the drink he went.

Unfortunately, by the time they'd fished the big shearer out, he was severely scalded to all parts of his body. Terrible it was, Old Jack reckoned. Definitely one of the worst cases of scalding he'd never seen.

But, to add to the tragedy, back in those days they didn't have doctors and nurses running around all over the place like they do today. So the only thing they could do to protect Big Ned was to take him back to his quarters and wrap him up into a swathe of freshly pulled sheepskins. Which they did.

Now they left these sheepskins on Big Ned for a month or so to allow the scalding to heal. But Old Jack said that when they tried to take the skins off, they found that they'd grafted onto him. Now there was no way that Big Ned was going to let his fleece get in the way of his shearing. He had a living to earn and, what's more, he loved shearing. So after that, before the start of each round of annual shearing, his mates had to run Big Ned in and they'd shear upwards of fifteen pound of wool off him before he was comfortable enough to start work.

And that's the real, true, fair-dinkum, ridgy-didge, authentic story of Big Ned from Big Burrawong, which was told to me by the most honest shearer you're ever likely not to meet, Old Jack. And, as Old Jack said to me in complete confidentiality, 'Anybody who has any doubts whatsoever about the authenticity of that story deserves a whack over the noggin with a hot bogghi.'

Oops-a-daisy

(Great Australian Railway Stories)

It was your typical bush town, set off the highway, with only two partly bituminised roads in and out of the place. One was coming in from the highway, going down the main street, past a couple of houses, our shop, the bank, then the pub, before dissolving into a dirt track and going out by the old church and heading off beside the railway line on its way to yet another smaller town. The other started out as a dirt track and it came in from some outlying wheat and sheep properties, past the footy oval, across the creek, before it turned into tar and went down, past a couple of houses and met the main street as a T-junction. Tucked into the undersides of the T-junction, and facing each other across the road, was the pub and the bank. If you went over the T-junction you'd end up in the gravel parking area of the railway station. Beyond that stood the silos.

Anyhow, each and every Saturday afternoon old Ted'd jump in his farm ute — one of those big, high-roofed things — and he'd drive from his farm, past the footy oval, over the creek, down the street to the T-junction and, more importantly, to the pub. Now he'd been doing this ever since I can remember and, ever since I can remember, he used to get as pissed as a newt each and every one of those Saturday nights.

But old Ted had worked out a strategy. See, because he knew he was going to get pissed, the first thing he did on his arrival in town was drive over the T-junction, into the gravel parking area of the railway station, do a U-ie, then drive back over the T-junction and park outside the bank which, as I mentioned, was over the street from the pub. With the ute now pointing in the direction of his home, he was safe in the knowledge that, later that night, he'd be able to stagger blindly outside, slip into the driver's seat, turn the key, start her up, and the ute'd head back down the street, across the creek, past the footy oval and down the dirt track, leading to his property. Of course, this'd been going on for so long that the locals used to joke about how old Ted's ute had more brains that what Ted did because it could drive its own way home.

Anyhow, we happened to own the shop that was beside the bank, which was across the road from the pub, and I remember the incident very clearly. I would've been — oh, I don't know — in that thirteen-to fourteen-year-old age bracket. I was in me early teen years, anyway. It was winter — footy season — and we must've had a home grand final because on that particular Saturday there were cars everywhere around the pub. So when old Ted arrived for his Saturday night piss-up he found all his usual spots were taken and he ended up having to park on the pub side of the road, which meant that his ute was pointing away from his home rather than towards it.

Now, it must've been quite late, about nine or ten o'clock at night. I was in me pyjamas, ready to go to bed, and Mum said, 'Shut the shop door up.' So I went out the front to shut the door and that's when I heard all this ruckus coming from over the pub.

And as you do when you're a kid, even on such a cold night as it was, I was drawn to the noise from the pub. But then, just as I got to the bank corner, old Ted's ute flashed by, heading in the wrong direction, and I watched as it went straight through the T-junction, straight into the railway yard, straight up the ramp, onto the platform and it crash-landed, nose first, down onto the railway line, leaving its back wheels hanging in midair.

So I run over to the pub to get Dad. 'Old Ted's just drove over the railway platform.' Of course, with everyone being well stonkered by that stage, I was met with calls of 'bullshit', or words to that effect. Anyhow, after a bit, they must've somehow realised that I was fair dinkum because they grabbed their beers and we all wandered over to the railway station. And sure enough, there was old Ted's ute, perched with its nose down on the railway tracks and its back wheels still spinning above the platform.

On surveying the situation, the blokes started scratching their heads and muttering swearwords and the like. Then someone clambered down from the platform, had a look in the cab of the ute and called out, 'Christ, old Ted's not here.' This caused a few more swearwords to be uttered until we heard old Ted's drunken voice coming from behind us. 'Oops-a-daisy, yer silly old coot. Oops-a-daisy, yer silly old coot.' And there's old Ted, he's sitting near one of those potted bushes that they always had on the railway stations and he's mumbling away to himself, 'Oops-a-daisy, yer silly old coot. Oops-a-daisy, yer silly old coot.'

Anyhow, the decision then had to be made as to the best way of dislodging the ute from off the railway platform and railway tracks. Of course, by this stage, with all these blokes having been in the pub for quite a few hours, old Ted wasn't the only one that was as pissed as a newt. They all were, so much so that I'd reckon if you popped the question as to who'd won that afternoon's grand final, the vast majority of them would've already forgotten. So when they all started trying to shout each other down with their own particular rescue plan for Ted's ute, the discussion soon turned into a complete rabble. But out from that rabble, a unanimous agreement was somehow reached that it'd very much help in the decision-making process if some more liquid refreshments were to be provided. So the publican went back over to the pub and brought back a crate of beer and everyone stood around and had another drink, while they tried to sort the problem out.

The first rescue plan decided upon was to pull the vehicle back up onto the railway platform. So someone got in the ute, started her up and stuck her in reverse, while the others gathered around ready to lift. That didn't work. The ute had back-wheel drive and, with the back wheels still being stuck 3 foot in the air, it was impossible for them to get any traction on the ground. What's more, with everyone having been weakened by the effects of the alcohol, the front of the ute proved too heavy to lift, anyway.

After the first effort had failed, the publican was sent back to the pub to get more liquid refreshments to help work things out. And it was while they were halfway through the second lot of beer that a train whistle pierced the night.

'Christ,' Dad shouted, 'that's the South West Mail. It was due through here yesterday.'

'Typical fuckin' railways,' someone replied.

Just then a bright light appeared down the railway track and a much louder whistle sounded and, in that instant, this group of men went from being as drunk as a mob of skunks into becoming as sober as a mob of judges. Someone dived into old Ted's ute, started it up and planted the accelerator. There was a crunch of gears and a howl from the engine. Smoke belched out from the exhaust. Wheels were spinning madly in the air. Blokes started pushing. Blokes started pulling. There were blokes shouting like crazy. Then another train whistle sounded and I was blinded by its bright lights.

I don't know exactly what happened next because I took off and hid in the ticket office. But I heard a lot of swearing. I heard a lot of crunching and banging. I smelt a lot of exhaust smoke and tyre rubber. Then, as the South West Mail thundered by, I heard a lot of cheering. And when I reappeared, the ute had somehow managed to escape to safety, over the far side of the railway line, heading toward the silos, and blokes were starting to gather back on the platform.

'I need a bloody drink,' someone said, which was a suggestion that was unanimously agreed upon.

So, without another word being said, they all wandered back over to the pub, leaving old Ted sitting by the potted bush, muttering, 'Oops-a-daisy, yer silly old coot. Oops-a-daisy, yer silly old coot.'

Roebourne — WA

(Great Australian Stories: Outback Towns and Pubs)

Hey, do they do police checks on these stories? Because I've got one here that could well land a mate of mine into a bit of hot water if they found out. See, back in me twenties, me and a couple of mates was doing the old 'around Australia trip'. We'd already crossed the Nullarbor to Perth and we were pretty skint and we'd heard there was work in Broome, so we're heading north and we came across a little town called Roebourne. Roebourne's on the road to Port Hedland. I can't remember too much about the place now other than there were a lot of Aboriginals living there; you know, around the streets and that, which was pretty typical in them sort of places.

Anyhow, it was around lunchtime and we decided to drop into the pub for a bite to eat and a beer or two. Good idea. So in we go. There were already a few locals in there — white fellers — and, even by that time of the day, they were pretty well on the way. Like, they'd had a few. It might've even been a weekend. Anyhow, we got talking to these fellers and somewhere along the line, one of me mates came across an idea. I mean, it sort of started out innocent enough, I guess, but I'll change the mate's name, just in case. Let's call him 'Bill', for argument's sake.

See, Bill was a fanatic punter. He used to punt like there was no tomorrow. He'd bet on two flies going up a wall if you gave him the right odds. He was that sort of feller. Anyhow, before we got to Roebourne we'd been staying a few hundred k's back down the track at Carnarvon and while we were there they'd run the English Derby; at Ascot, I think it was. There might've even been an Australian horse running in it or something. I don't know. But, see, seeing how the English Derby was run during our Australian night-time, Bill had recorded it all on his big, new, fandangle radio-tape recorder so he could listen to it more closely the next day, when he was sober.

So we're drinking with these Roebourne fellers and Bill takes a sudden look at his watch and said, 'Geez, the English Derby's on in a tick. I might go 'n' have a listen to it on me portable radio.'

Now, as I said, these blokes were pretty well gone so I don't know if they even twigged that the English Derby had already been run or not and, if they did, they'd forgot. But, whatever the caper, they said, all excited like, 'Oh, bring yer radio in 'ere so we can all 'ave a listen.'

So Bill went out to the car and he got his radio-tape player and he put in the tape of the English Derby and he brought it back into the pub and set it up on the bar and there's all these blokes gathered around, primed up, ready to listen to this race. So Bill pretends to turn the radio on, but instead he starts the tape going and the Pommy race caller comes on and he's going through the horse's names and giving out their starting prices and that. Now, I'm not sure whether Bill'd actually planned all this out or not but, when a few of the Roebourne boys started reckoning to each other what horse would win, Bill piped up and said, 'Who wants ter lay a bet?'

'Me. Me. Me,' all these fellers said.

'I'll take the odds, then,' says Bill, and when the race caller gave out the final starting-price fluctuations — you know, which horse's odds were shortening and which horse's odds were lengthening — Bill got to work, making sure that whenever someone wanted to place a bet on the winner-to-be, he halved its starting price.

Anyhow, when the race started, there's all these Roebourne fellers — pissed as newts — around this radio-tape player, all yelling and hooting and going on, trying to bring home the horse they'd put their money on. And, actually, Bill ended up making a tidy sum out of that little caper and that's about all I can tell you about Roebourne because we buggered off out of there pretty soon after that.

Kicking the Dust

(The Complete Book of Australian Flying Doctor Stories)

Well, it's all just been pretty predictable stuff really. The evacuations that we've had to make out of here have gone off pretty much without a hitch. By 'here' I'm meaning Mount Vernon Station which is north of Meekatharra, in the central east of Western Australia.

Anyway, it's always amazed me how the Flying Doctor has been able to get in and out in quick-smart time. They're pretty efficient, you know, the lot of them — the doctors, the nurses, the pilots. We haven't even had any high-flaunting dramas about aeroplanes getting bogged in the bulldust or the mud like they have at other places. Still and all, there was one time I remember when the Flying Doctor plane was delayed from leaving our place, and that was for a bit of an odd sort of reason really, so I'll tell you about that one if you like.

As I said, the Flying Doctor plane has been able to get in and out in no time at all apart from this occasion when a young lad, a jackaroo he was, came off his horse and got his foot caught in the stirrup. Gee, he was in a mess. The poor kid had been dragged along the ground for a fair way and, among all that, the horse had trampled over him. I tell you, he was a pretty bruised and battered young man.

Anyway, we sent out an emergency for the Flying Doctor. When the plane arrived, on board was a doctor, a pilot and a nursing sister. So they settled the young stockman down and had just loaded him onto the plane when the nursing sister decided that she'd better go to the toilet before they flew back to the Meekatharra base.

'Sure,' I said and directed her off to the nearest loo, an outside construction it was. 'You go down this way and that, and it's just around the corner, over there, in that direction.'

Now one of the peculiarities of this particular toilet was that it had a metal door. So, when the sun shone on it, the metal expanded. Of course, we knew this and whenever we used the toilet we kept the door slightly open. But the nursing sister didn't, and with all the kerfuffle over the young stockman it completely slipped my mind to tell her. To make matters worse, this was a warm day, a very warm day indeed.

So off she went and the doctor completed what was necessary for the young stockman while the pilot did his pre-take-off checks. Some time passed and the nursing sister still hadn't returned. So there we were, standing around, trying to fill in the time with idle chat. And we waited and we waited until eventually we'd just about exhausted every avenue of conversation from the price of beef right through to the current climatic conditions ... and still she hadn't appeared.

By this stage, the patient was looking quite distressed, the poor kid. What's more, the doctor seemed pretty anxious and the pilot was gazing at his watch then up at the skies then back at his watch again. So there we were, hovering around the plane kicking the dust with our boots, trying to think of what to talk about next, which we couldn't because all the while we were wondering what the hell was going on with the nursing sister.

Anyway, all this tension proved too much for my husband. 'Oh gee,' he blurted, 'I don't know, perhaps she isn't feeling too well.'

With this comment, the men turned to me. Being a female I put two and two together and came up with the obvious — that they weren't too comfortable about knocking on a toilet door to find out what a woman's problem might be.

'I'd better go and check on her, then,' I said.

'Good idea,' they chorused.

So I went over to the toilet and tapped on the door. 'Excuse me,' I said, 'but are you okay in there?'

'I'm in big trouble,' came the plaintive reply.

'What's up?' I asked, thinking the worst.

'The door's stuck and I can't get out.'

So I had a go at opening the thing and it was stuck, all right, stuck good and proper. What's more, it wouldn't budge no matter how hard I tried. Then I had to call the men around to have a go. God it was funny. If you can imagine the scene, there we were out in the middle of nowhere with these three men huffing and puffing and pushing and pulling at the door of the toilet which in turn was causing the complete structure to sway back and forward, and there was this poor woman stuck inside thinking that all her nightmares had come at once.

But they eventually managed to free it.

'One, two, three,' they called and gave an almighty pull.

The toilet door flung open and out stepped one very embarrassed nursing sister — as red as a beetroot, she was.

'Well,' she snapped, 'shall we go then?' And she strode off in the direction of the plane.

Stone the Crows

(Great Australian Railway Stories)

It's very different now but, back in them days, not only all the railway's communications but also all the telephone communications and ABC telecommunications were carried across the Nullarbor by a series of wires strung between telephone poles, which ran beside the railway track. Anyway, because there's no trees on the Nullarbor — in fact, the word Nullarbor means 'no trees' — the crows used to build their nests on the wooden cross arms of these telephone poles. And they were a real bugbear on communications because the nests actually formed what's called a 'loop', and that could bugger the system up quite bad.

Anyhow, a young feller came out through our railway camp, one day. He had a very rich accent so I knew straightaway he was English. He was new to the area so I asked what he was doing and he said he was a linesman. Now, predominantly, a linesman's job was to inspect the telephone poles to make sure the cross arms weren't broken plus other general maintenance. So I said to this Pom, 'Oh, that's good. How long have yer been on the job?'

'Only a couple of weeks,' he said.

Of course, straightaway, being who I am, I said, 'What're yer gonna do?'

'Well, in fact,' he said, 'I've been told by my boss to make sure that I clear the crows' nests off the cross arms.'

Now I knew the boss guy who was in charge of all these linesmen very, very well, you know, so I just hesitated for a second then I said, 'Have yer ever had anything to do with crows before?'

'No, no,' he said. 'But apparently they're much like our English ravens, aren't they?'

'Well, yes, they may look a bit like ravens,' I said, 'but I tell you what, when they're nesting, they're bloody ferocious birds. You want'a be very, very careful because if you start pulling down their nests, they'll bloody attack yer, no doubt about it,' I said. 'They've even been known to kill fellers.'

Of course, I promptly forgot about this little interlude and the Pommy linesman went off to do his thing and I went back to my job, and it must've been, oh, I don't know, six months or so later, when this Pommy feller's boss rang me. He said, 'When you're in bloody town next, mate,' he said, 'I want'a talk to you.'

So next time I was in town I went around to see him and he said, 'What did you tell that bloody Pommy bloke of mine about them crows?' So I told him and he said, 'You stupid bastard,' he said. 'Do you know what you've done? You put the wind up that poor kid so much that he was too scared to go near any of them crows' nests and now the whole bloody communications system's up the bloody creek.'

Blue Hills

(Great Australian Shearing Stories)

Now here's a story from the 1950s that demonstrates typical bush humour. As you might remember, that was the era of the famous radio serial *Blue Hills*. Just about everybody used to listen to that show back then, especially the people from the bush. It became a part of their lives.

So I was about eighteen at that time, and the boss on this sheep property where I worked was a very highly strung sort of bloke. It got on your goat because he was so — what's the word? — pedantic, finicky, like. Everything always had to go strictly to plan — his plan in particular. Everything had to be done his way.

Anyhow, this time the boss was anxious to get the shearing under way. The only trouble was, old Bill the shearer hadn't turned up. In them days Bill drove about with his shearing plant in the back of his ute and he was supposed to have been there and started by 7.30am, on the dot. But already it was after eight. Then, to make matters worse, the weather was threatening and, as you'd know, if the sheep get wet, they don't shear, and that was the last thing the boss wanted to happen. So there he was, the boss, stamping around as cranky as all heck.

Now old Bill was a renowned stirrer and he never let a chance go by to pull a leg or two. So Bill finally rolled up with his two-stander roped down in the back of his ute and he backed her up to the old thatched woolshed. The boss by this stage was hovering close by, fidgeting about, mumbling under his breath. Now old Bill, of course, immediately sensed the boss's agitation. 'Here's a go,' he thought. So he eased himself out of his ute, scratched his bum, looked up at the sky and began to shake his head in a very concerned sort of manner.

'Ah, jeez,' he said to no one in particular, but making sure that the boss was within earshot. 'I don't know about this. Looks like rain.'

At that comment the boss's mouth sprung open and he was just about to give Bill a spray, to hurry him along, like, but then he shut it again, very quick. See, the boss knew that if he upset old Bill in any way that he'd just pack up and leave, which meant that the boss would've been left without a sheep being shorn, and no shearer to do the shearing.

So old Bill wandered around his ute, kicking the tyres here and there as he carefully undid the ropes that were holding the shearing plant down. The boss, meanwhile, looked up at the threatening sky and began to pace back and forward in a frantic fashion. But that didn't seem to concern old Bill. He just idled along as if he had all the time in the world. Then, when he finally undid all the ropes, we helped him lift the plant off the tray of the ute and set it up in the shed. 'There,' said old Bill, with a sigh of satisfaction at a job well done.

But, when he tried to start the machine, for some unknown reason it wouldn't go. So old Bill looked at the machine, scratched his head for a while, then he wandered back to his ute to get a few spanners, a few screwdrivers, and a mallet out of his toolbox. When he came back he had another think, a bit of a scratch, then gave the machine a hefty smack around the backside with the mallet and, lo and behold, it spluttered into action.

'Well,' he said, with a sideways glance at the boss, 'that's fixed that.'

Then with a look at his watch, he turned the machine off, walked back to his ute and he took out a thermos and a lunchbox.

'What the bloody ...' the boss said, about to blow his top.

'It's me smoko,' old Bill interrupted. 'A bloke's gotta have 'is smoko.'

Which he did. Old Bill settled down to have his smoko. First he opened his lunchbox and began to chew thoughtfully on a sandwich. 'Beautiful,' he said aloud. 'The missus makes beautiful sandwiches, she does.'

Then he poured out a mug of black tea from his thermos, took a sip, and called out, 'Beautiful. The missus makes a beautiful cuppa tea.'

As you might imagine, this wasn't going down too well with the boss at all. The storm clouds were gathering rapidly. Precious time was slipping by and the boss's blood pressure was nearing boiling point.

So, after he'd devoured his sandwiches and downed his tea, old Bill packed the thermos and lunchbox back into the ute.

'Gotta sharpen up me gear,' he announced. 'Had to leave the last place in a bit of a hurry.'

Then he set up his grinding wheel and began to sharpen his gear, ready for the day's work. After that he decided that he had to oil the gear. Then he put his leather apron on, sorted out his handpiece, and laid it out all nice and neat.

Finally, much to the relief of the boss, old Bill loosened his shoulders in preparation for a hard day's work and he turned the motor on. Then, just as he was about to go into the pen to grab the first sheep of the day, he glanced at his watch, rushed back over, and he switched the machine off again.

By this time it's midday. Not one sheep's been shorn. There's thunder echoing in the background. And the boss, well, he'd had enough.

'What the bloody hell are you stopping the plant for now!' he bellowed.

'Jeez boss,' old Bill replied with all the calm in the world. '*Blue Hills* is on in a tick. I gotta listen to that.'

Then the boss stormed out of the shed and we never saw him again for the rest of the day.

Speared

(More Great Australian Flying Doctor Stories)

Well, I joined the Flying Doctor Service in 1989. That was as a pilot out at Meekatharra, which is in the central west of Western Australia. Then, after about six months at Meekatharra, in early May 1990 I went to work up at their Port Hedland base. I stayed at Port Hedland then for thirteen years, until 2003, and oh, we loved it there. We had a young family and it was such a good, safe place to bring up kids. We also loved camping so there was lots of bush trips and travelling around the Pilbara and the Kimberley. The Gibb River Road's one of my favourite places in Australia. Actually, I think we've done the Gibb River Road about six times and I reckon there's still more to see. Fabulous country up that way. In fact, just about my whole flying career has taken place throughout the tropical areas of Australia. You know, northern Western Australia right across to northern Queensland.

But as far as stories go, you always sort of have your favourites, don't you? One that I think was quite amusing in an odd sort of way — well, both sad and amusing, I guess — happened at Jigalong Aboriginal Community. Jigalong's about 120 kilometres east of the mining town of Newman, in central Western Australia.

Anyhow, once every two or three years the Indigenous folk conduct what's called Law Ceremonies. Now, these Law Ceremonies happen when all the various communities from within the wider area gather together in a designated community and, along with a lot of celebrations, the Elders review events since the last get-together. So they'd do things like the initiations with the young boys who haven't yet been initiated, and also they'd deal out the tribal punishment for any misdemeanours or whatever that may have occurred over the last couple of years or so. So you could do something wrong and then you might have to wait for a year or more before you got punished, in the appropriate law time.

On this particular occasion there'd been a car roll over and two passengers had been killed and so the driver of the vehicle was brought before the Elders. The Elders listened to what had happened and deemed that it was the driver's fault for causing the deaths of the two others. So he had to be punished and the Elders said that his punishment was to be a stabbing in the thigh, by a spear.

So a few men grabbed hold of the bloke who'd been driving the car and they held him as still as they could, ready to receive the punishment. But apparently the driver bloke was wriggling and turning and writhing around so much that the enforcer of the punishment clean missed his mark and he ended up spearing the driver bloke in the lower abdomen instead of the thigh.

That's when we got an emergency call to go out there to Jigalong Community to pick up the bloke who'd been speared. The only trouble was that, unfortunately, it'd been raining heavily over the area for the past week or so and there was no way we could land the aeroplane on Jigalong airstrip.

But, seeing that it was an emergency, they arranged to charter a helicopter from Karratha. The helicopter was then flown up to Newman and we took the RFDS aeroplane down from Port Hedland, where we all got into the helicopter and we flew out from Newman to Jigalong. Along with the helicopter pilot we took the normal complement of RFDS staff, which was a doctor, the nurse and myself.

And so we went out in the chartered helicopter and landed at the local oval, at Jigalong Community, and they brought out the poor guy who'd been inadvertently speared in the lower abdomen. We quickly laid him on the stretcher, put him onto the helicopter and took him back to Newman. The helicopter then headed back to Karratha and we put the speared bloke into the RFDS aeroplane and flew him back to Port Hedland, where he was going to be treated.

Then we'd only just arrived back in Port Hedland when we got another call asking us to return to Jigalong Community. Apparently, what happened was that the Elders had gone and handed out another punishment and that person had been speared, this time in the thigh. Anyhow, I think that in the end they decided that this new bloke's wounds weren't quite bad enough to warrant us going through the whole procedure again. You know — of chartering another helicopter to fly out there and for us to fly down to Newman, and all that. I mean, the cost was astronomical. I'd estimate that just that one retrieval cost would've been well over $30,000.

But the irony of the whole thing was that we later found out that the second call for us to return to Jigalong Community was to pick up the bloke who'd inadvertently stuffed up the first spearing. Apparently the Elders deemed that he should be punished for being such a poor shot.

Normanton — Qld

(Great Australian Stories: Outback Towns and Pubs)

To give you some idea, the Carpentaria Shire is as large as Tasmania. So it's pretty big, and there's always been a large Aboriginal population, not only in Normanton itself, but also throughout the entire Gulf region. Then, the first European to navigate the Norman River was William Landsborough. That was in early 1867, and on that trip he chose the site of the township and just a few months later the first settlers arrived, more or less as pastoralists. But Normanton really came into its own as a supply port, when gold was discovered around the Croydon area, a couple of years later. They'd bring the gold here and ship it out, down the fifty-six mile, to the river mouth at Karumba. And so, between Normanton and Croydon is where they have the historic train, The Gulflander. The building of that began in the late 1880s and the original steel sleepers, track, station and goods sheds remain, making it the oldest original rail line in Australia, if not the world, still in use today.

After the gold rush, Normanton settled down, the population dropped, and it returned to being a pretty sleepy sort of place. And that's the way everyone liked it. So, I guess, like so many other small towns, the locals got used of each other's company and newcomers were viewed with a large degree of suspicion until they'd somehow proved themselves. Take Rita Pointon for instance. She turned up here in the early 1950s to take over as Matron at the hospital and no-one wanted to be the first to visit her. Not until she'd proven herself, anyway. So everyone just stayed at home and put up with their illnesses, aches and pains and grumbles. And it wasn't till things were starting to get a bit desperate on the health front that someone turned up at the hospital with a horse — a foal — and said, 'Matron, me horse's crook, can yer do somethin' for it?'

Now, I don't know what was wrong with this foal but, with nothing better to do, Rita took it into her care. Then everyone waited in eager anticipation for the outcome. You know, if it lived or died. Well it did live, and the day after Rita released the now healthy horse from hospital she was met by a waiting room full of people, with all sorts of ailments. And, back in those days, the matron had to do everything. She was the doctor, the nurse, she pulled teeth, stitched people up. She set broken legs, the lot. So I guess you could say that Rita had 'passed muster' and from then on she was accepted. In fact, during her nineteen years as Matron, she become a very much loved person throughout the community. A true legend.

Then they built the new hospital in about 1984. That's where I worked as a Registered Nurse, and that's where this story took place just over twenty years ago. Anyhow, this particular night I was rostered on with a male nurse's aide by the name of Jacko. Jacko was a real character. He'd lived and worked in Normanton for many years so he knew everyone and everyone knew him. There was never a dull moment. He was always full of energy and fun. Staff and patients alike loved him and he could make even the sourest person smile and feel good about themselves. A top nurse's aide. Totally efficient. Great to work with. And he called a spade a spade. There was no beating about the bush with Jacko. Anyhow, there was only ever two staff on duty for a night shift and around midnight myself and Jacko, we had a call to the front door where we found a drunken woman, doubled up, apparently in severe pain. Now, I don't know which hotel she'd been drinking in because there's three pubs in Normanton. There's what everyone calls the Top Pub, which is the National. Then there's the Middle Pub, which is the Central. Then there's the Bottom Pub, the Albion. Now, as it turned out, Jacko knew the woman from somewhere. Like I said, Jacko knew everyone. Anyhow, we helped her into the hospital and up onto an examination table. We didn't know what was wrong but she was moaning and groaning and going on about how bad the pain was and also that her and her de facto, who was apparently also drunk, they'd had a blue and, as she told us, 'He's gonna get me, good 'n' proper, missus. Says he's gonna kill me.'

By then we had a doctor working at the hospital. The only trouble was that the poor fellow was on call every day and night of the week. If he was lucky he might get four or five days off a month, but that's only if a relieving doctor could be found. And relieving doctors were as scarce as hens' teeth. Anyhow, after taking the usual vital signs and observations, it was still hard to assess this woman's problem, so we decided to call the doctor. He arrived, tired and strung out, and after an initial examination he decided he'd need to examine the patient further. He was a very prim and proper fellow, very committed to his work, even at all times of the day or, in this case, the night. Anyhow, so that he could have a more thorough investigation of the patient, he decided that a rectal examination was necessary. So he said to the patient, 'Excuse me,' he said, 'would you mind turning over on your side so that I can examine you more thoroughly?'

The woman didn't have a clue what he was on about and so she answered with an abrupt and drunken, 'Ay?'

'Well,' said the doctor, 'I need you to turn over on your side, please, because I'd like to do a P.R. examination.'

'A what?'

So the doctor tried to make it clearer by saying, 'Look, I'm afraid that I have to do a rectal examination to more closely assess your condition.'

The woman was still confused so she turned to Jacko. 'Hey, Jacko,' she slurred, 'what's this bastard talkin' about?'

As quick as a flash, Jacko replied, 'Oh, don't worry, he just wants ter stick his finger up yer arse.'

Well, what a miraculous recovery. 'Fuck that,' the woman shouted and she was down and off the table in a flash and she took off down the corridor, screaming out about how she'd be better off dealing with her de facto's threat of killing her than having some stranger stick his finger up her behind.

And as the woman scampered out of the building, the doctor turned to Jacko and said, 'Well, Jacko, you certainly have a wonderful way with words, mate.'

Fucked

(Great Australian Bush Funeral Stories)

I think I may have mentioned this incident back when we were talking about my nursing experiences. But anyway, whatever, it's quite a unique tale in its way and may well fit into your gatherings of funeral-type stories.

Just a bit of background first: I grew up in Brisbane, so I guess you could say I was a city girl. Though, due to my father's rewarding occupation, we were fortunate enough to also own a small property outside of the city. That's where we'd spend most of our weekends, and so maybe it's why I originally wanted to go jillarooing. But no, my parents were dead against me going bush. They wanted me to have something more solid behind me.

So, not wanting to have a job where I'd end up sitting behind a desk, putting on weight, I decided to give nursing a go. And as soon as I started my training, that was it: nursing was the be-all and end-all of it. From that moment on, nursing's all I've ever wanted to do. I did my three years of general nursing training in Maryborough, which is up in the Fraser Coast area, about two hundred and fifty kilometres north of Brisbane. Following that I did twelve months of midwifery at a place just a hundred k's north of Brisbane, called Nambour. After those postings I wanted to spread my wings a bit and so I decided to go over to the Northern Territory and work in intensive care in Alice Springs Hospital.

Alice Springs was really my first big job out of training. We're now talking about the late '80s. I was still quite young and naive and there I was working in ICU — the intensive care unit. And

I can tell you, what a massive cultural learning curve that was. Up until then I'd had very little to do with Aboriginal people and now, suddenly, being in Alice Springs, I was right in the thick of it. A large number of those who came to the hospital were local Indigenous people and so they were quite urbanised, if I can use that phrase. But then there were those from the outlying mission communities who were still living in a more traditional manner. With most of the ones from the outlying communities being non-English speaking, the first difficulty I faced was how to communicate with them. Right from the start I had to learn the basic cultural things, like how a woman wasn't allowed to look an Aboriginal man in the eyes and how you were to bow your head when you were talking to a male, particularly an Elder.

But after I'd got over the initial shock, I actually found it really fascinating. I remember the time when one of the community clinic doctors flew an Indigenous male in to us. When the man arrived in ICU he was unconscious. When we checked him out there was nothing untoward in his pathology, nor were there any obvious indications of injury or disease. We then managed to get the story from his family that he'd recently married a woman who was outside of his tribe. With this being very much against their particular culture, his wife's tribe had organised a kurdaitcha man to 'sing' him to death.

Now I guess you could liken a kurdaitcha man to someone that we'd describe as a witch doctor. They're the ones that can wield magic. And I don't know if your readers would also be aware of this or not, but a 'singing' in Aboriginal culture is similar to having a bone pointed at you. In basic terms it's like scaring someone to death by putting a curse on them for doing something wrong within tribal law. In fact, it's an amazing mix of cultural superstition, magic and imagination.

Anyhow, we put this man who'd been sung on the ventilator to keep him breathing and we gave him intravenous fluids to keep up his nutrition. But we were getting nowhere. He was just lying there, unconscious, with no improvement or deterioration to his current condition. After a discussion between the doctors and some of the local Elders, it was decided to send a small clinic plane back out to the man's community and bring in their tribe's own specially strong kurdaitcha man to see what he could do. The thinking there was that he might be able to use his magical powers to somehow override the curse that had been put on the man who'd been sung.

When this special kurdaitcha man arrived, he was all done up in his full regalia and ready to go. He'd not only brought along some sort of special stones and crystals but he was also literally covered in feathers. I tell you, he had feathers on his arms, on his ankles, on his wrists and on his head. He even wore a skirt of feathers and there was a mass of larger feathers plus an assortment of bones hanging around his neck, like a necklace. Then, before he went in to see the man, he requested that the room be darkened. So we turned all the lights off and we hung curtains over the windows. After we'd done that, we were told that we all had to leave the room and go and wait outside.

So I don't know what actually went on with the feathers and the stones and the crystals along with the occasional chant and grunt and groan that emanated out of the room but, some time later, the kurdaitcha man reappeared.

'How did you go?' one of the doctors asked.

'No good,' the kurdaitcha man replied. 'He's fucked.' Then he brushed straight past us, walked down the hallway and out of the hospital and he was taken back out to the airport to be flown back to his community. And that was that. Our poor patient was even beyond help from this extra-strong kurdaitcha man.

Of course, the doctors were still quite sceptical about all this. In fact, one of them mentioned how it was all a load of bullshit, and so we continued to monitor the man and feed him and artificially breathe for him with the ventilator. But still no change.

Then a day or so after the kurdaitcha man had returned to his community, all these old, battered and bashed-up vehicles pulled up outside the hospital, packed to the hilt with members of the patient's family and tribe. There would've been at least fifty of them. Now I just can't quite remember what community they were from, but they'd driven a long way — hundreds of kilometres. Anyhow, they all piled out of their vehicles and into the ICU they filed to take up their positions, sitting down along the corridor, outside the man's room. And then they started wailing. And they wailed and they wailed for a full twenty-four hours.

And these people weren't shushed or asked to leave. Hospital policy was to allow them their cultural right to go through their traditional grieving process — and the other patients in the ICU just had to bear it. But the thing was, throughout this process, not one of them got up and went into the room to see the man, not even any of his relatives. They all just sat there in the corridor and they wailed and they wailed. I'll never forget it. It was the most eerie of sounds I've ever heard. Absolutely chilling.

Then the strangest of things happened. Just as the wailing reached its crescendo, the man passed away. And with no one else in his room bar us, there was no way that the man's actual passing could've been known by any of his tribe. But at the exact moment the ECG monitor flatlined, they all got up and they walked out of the hospital. Just like that, and that was the end of it. We couldn't believe it. We just stood there, aghast. The man had been sung to death. So the special kurdaitcha man's diagnosis had been spot on. 'He's fucked,' he'd said, and the poor man was.

Amazing isn't it?

See Yer Later

(The Complete Book of Australian Flying Doctor Stories)

Now, I've only got just the one Flying Doctor story, so I don't know if it's of use to you.

Okay, well some years ago, after exploring Ningaloo Reef, between Exmouth and Coral Bay, which is up in the northern coastal region of Western Australia, we headed off to Exmouth Airport, with our dive bags and packs, to catch a small plane to Broome. When we arrived at Exmouth, there were only a couple of four-wheel drives in the airport car park. Then, further to that, we discovered that the actual terminal was completely deserted; that is, except for one bloke who was behind a check-in counter.

'G'day,' we said.

'Oh, glad you've turned up,' he beamed. 'You're the only passengers for the day!'

'What? No one else here?' I asked.

'No,' he replied, 'just the bloke in the Control Tower.' Then he gave us the tags to stick on our luggage. 'Here,' he said, 'stick these on your bags and have a good flight.'

Which we did and then, to our surprise, he slipped under the counter and headed out to the car park. So we settled into these terribly bright red seats that were in the waiting lounge. To give you some idea, they were a kind of a cross between a beanbag and a park bench-seat. In actual fact, the whole terminal was done out in probably what some people would call 'post-modern'. But at least the windows were huge, even if the runway and tarmac were totally deserted.

So, anyway, we sat and we waited. And we sat and we waited, and the departure time for our six-seater came and went. Then eventually we heard a plane. As the plane landed and taxied to the terminal, we read 'Royal Flying Doctor Service' on the side of it. Of course, this obviously wasn't our Broome service. Anyhow, the instant the engines died a young woman dressed in uniform jumped out of the plane and she started running towards the terminal. At seeing her urgency and sensing an emergency, I went over to meet her at the gateway.

'I'm sorry,' I said, 'but we're the only people here, except for the bloke in the Control Tower.'

'No worries,' she said, 'I'm just busting for a piss.' And she keep on running, straight towards the toilet.

So I went and sat back down again. Then she emerged a little later, looking far more relaxed, and she walked sedately over to us.

'So where are you going?' she asked.

'Broome,' we said.

'Bad luck,' she said, 'we're heading the other way.'

'Oh,' we said.

Then she said, 'See yer later then,' and rushed back out to the RFDS plane, jumped back in, and they took off.

The Discovery

(Swampy)

She was a runt of a kid really. Born with some mystery disease which caused her parents to force-feed her with gallons and gallons of goat's milk.

It showed. Her hair was white and soft, like goat's fleece.

Her name was Bewler Saunders. She came from next door. We used to let her join in our games, because no other girls lived close to town. She proved handy at fetching cricket balls from out of the drains and stuff. She was also good for a laugh, so we didn't mind her tagging along.

One scorching summer's day she was with Brownie, McCaughney and me down the creek, snake hunting. We'd recently had a good flush of water through and in one spot a nice muddy swimming hole remained.

Bewler suggested we all go for a skinny dip. She took off her clothes and dived in.

It was at that moment it struck me that the difference between boys and girls is that girls don't have anything between their legs. And I'm sure it wasn't only me that this discovery suddenly hit, because Brownie and McCaughney also appeared stunned at that sight of nothingness. Within a flash we boys had stripped off and were splashing around in the water with this girl, who'd now become the strange object of our fascination.

Unbeknown to us all, by the time we were clambering out of that evaporating water hole, our friendships had changed. Without one single word having been uttered, new ground rules had been set. Bewler became a spectator of our games and was never asked to fetch balls. It was us boys who fought tooth and nail to find that ball, then proudly display it in Bewler's direction, shouting: 'I found it! I found it!'

Our male competitive instincts grew to enormous proportions. While the victor sat high upon his pedestal, the defeated, tears welling in their eyes, lay shattered upon the dusty battlefield.

As we bickered, snarled and snapped amongst ourselves, we showered Bewler with gifts of plastic rings, boiled lollies, hidden love messages, sherbets and crushed flowers.

She fell in the school playground, grazing her knee. Opening her pain out to the sky, she cried. Upon hearing her plea for help, we dropped bats, balls and gloves mid-Test Match to rush to the side of our princess in her hour of need. I was the fastest runner and reached her first. But Brownie began to argue that he'd reached her first. Then McCaughney said we were both wrong, and that he was first upon the scene. This was a complete lie because everyone knows that McCaughney is as slow as a wet week.

The fight that ensued left us with bloodied noses, black eyes, sore knuckles and a barrage of questions to be answered.

'Why suddenly all this fighting? You were all such good friends once. Who started it all?' asked the schoolmaster.

None of us was prepared to admit that our whole world had been changed from day to night, with the discovery of a girl.

Fights began breaking out over such little things as who had the best lunch, who could throw further, who knew the most swear words. When Brownie announced one day that he'd 'kissed Bewler Saunders', McCaughney and I gave him the belting of his life, before heading off to find that girl of such bad taste and demand our equal reward.

Mine was given behind the wood heap. Crouched uncomfortably amongst the mallee roots, sawn gum and redback spiders. My heart pumping so loud I was sure Bewler could hear it.

Lips tightly puckered, we advanced and squashed our faces together. I smelt the waxy flavour of goat's milk. I closed my eyes, awaiting the orchestra that Mum heard when Dad first kissed her.

The chooks went about their business nonchalantly around us. I pushed into Bewler's face as hard as I could. My teeth about splitting my tightly shut lips. We sat adhesived to each other.

Time evaporated as the hot sun passed in the sky. I waited. I began to pick the next Australian Cricket team ... in alphabetical order. My stomach rumbled ... I tried to guess what Mum'd cook for tea.

Then I opened my eyes. Bewler's eyes were already opened. I noticed that they were blue and looked bored. We parted apologetically.

'Was I any good?' she asked.

I looked at a mallee root and mumbled through my swollen lips, 'Beaut.'

Then she said, 'Gee, I hope I don't have a baby.'

* * *

Well I didn't eat any tea that night nor the next. I began to renew my lost friendship with God, pleading my case of ignorance deep into the small hours. I promised I'd follow the Christian doctrine until my dying day and obey my parents' every order, without whimper or argument. I'd do anything just as long as Bewler didn't have my baby.

Unasked, I washed dishes, brushed shoes, did my homework, cleaned my teeth ... all to prove to God that I was fair dinkum.

My school marks rose. My cricket average plummeted. I was troubled.

Gathering enough courage, I asked Dad how long it takes to know if someone's going to have a baby. He told me to ask my mother. Mum said, 'A month or two.'

I prayed harder than ever. Louder than ever. Longer than ever. And God heard me. Because Bewler didn't swell up when the two months was up. That dark cloud of pending fatherhood lifted. I was free.

My cricket average rose. My school marks plummeted. I was happy.

Once more I could look the world, and everyone, square in the eye. Except Bewler, of course. Our relationship had passed.

* * *

The following year, Brownie, McCaughney and me returned to that place in the creek where we'd swum naked with a girl. In idle manly boast, I skited that Bewler almost had my baby ... Then Brownie said that she almost had his baby ... McCaughney said the same thing ...

We sat, once again united in our mateship, looking as one into that now dried creek bed, wondering if girls would ever have anything more exciting to offer us; other than dry, painful kisses, pregnancy scares ... and nothing between their legs.

Barton — SA

(Great Australian Stories: Outback Towns and Pubs)

Now Barton's an interesting little place. Ever heard of it? Not many have. It's away out on the Nullarbor, in South Australia, at the start of the world's longest straight stretch of railway track, leading from there to eternity then further on to Kalgoorlie, in Western Australia. There's bugger-all there these days apart from flies and a fluctuating population of somewhere between one and ten, and that's counting the wild horses and stray camels. Even for the most imaginative of real estate agents the best that could be said about the place is that it's 'nestled comfortably among endless rolling red sandhills'. Beyond that, you'd be scratching.

Anyhow, back a few years the railways scaled down and there was an old German bloke, by the name of Ziggie, who worked as a fettler out there. With all the kerfuffle, Ziggie decided to chuck it in after thirty years on the job. But instead of retiring to the Big Smoke of Port Augusta, like the rest of the workers out that way tended to do, he thought, 'Vell, bugger it. I haft seven dogs, novere to go. Zo as-t long as-t zee Tea an' Sugar Train still delivers vater an' supplies, I'll stay in zee Barton.' Ziggie loved his dogs.

The trouble was that he and the dogs had been left with no place to live and so for the next couple of years he wandered up and down the track picking up the sleepers that had been cast aside during track maintenance. And out of those he built a huge three-roomed bunker, complete with a patio, where he and his dogs could sit and sip on their Milo and watch the sun set over the endlessly rolling sandhills. Now you may think that the mention of Ziggie sipping on Milo instead of a gin and tonic or a cold beer was a slip of the tongue. But it wasn't. Ziggie drank nothing but Milo. In actual fact, his staple diet was Milo, oranges, potatoes and, as the strong rumour had it, dog food. Yep, you heard it right ... Milo, oranges, potatoes and dog food for breakfast, dinner and tea, and a good brand it was too.

So Ziggie settled down to life at Barton and, believe me, he just happened to be one of the best informed individuals that you're ever likely to meet. As you might imagine, there wasn't too much else for him to do out there except listen to his short-wave radio. So Ziggie got to know more about the goings-on of the world than anyone I've known. What's more, he had an opinion on any subject, and if he didn't he'd soon make one up.

So it was a pretty solitary affair out at Barton which, in turn, caused the few Bartonites who also lived there to get extremely suspicious when a blow-in lobbed in town. Not that many did, mind you. Maybe one or two each decade or so. But that was just enough for the locals, including Ziggie, to have formed the solid opinion that the rest of the world was inhabited by weirdos. And so it was when one of the locals wandered out at the crack of dawn one day and discovered that some bloke, a blow-in, had appeared from God-knows-where in the middle of the night and had been bowled over by the Tea and Sugar Train as it was pulling into the siding. The evidence was right there for all to see. There was this complete stranger, sprawled under the front of the train, out to the world, comatose in fact, with his head split open, stinking of grog and looking at death's door.

'Typical, ay?' one Bartonite muttered, to which there was total agreement.

Of course, the train driver was upset. But as he said, 'How the hell could I have bowled someone over when the train only travels at snail's pace?' And there were those who understood what he was on about. See, it'd been rumoured that the driver of the Tea and Sugar Train was given a calendar, rather than a timetable, upon departure from Port Augusta because it could never be guaranteed as to what actual time of the day he arrived at Kalgoorlie, it was more like what month of the year it was.

Anyhow, naturally, not long after Ziggie and his dogs arrived upon the scene of the accident, Ziggie had come up with his own theory. He reckoned that the train hadn't hit the blow-in but that the bloke had been so pissed, when he'd staggered out of the sandhills at some ungodly hour of the night, he'd inadvertently walked headlong into the stationary train. Crack! Split his head open and down he'd gone like a sack of spuds, right under the front wheels, and hadn't moved a muscle since.

But, theory or no theory, the bloke was in a bad way and so someone got in touch with the Flying Doctor Service at Port Augusta. 'We'll be there in an hour,' they said, and then, while they were waiting for the RFDS plane to arrive, a healthy discussion raged as to why the hell the blow-in had been wandering out in the desert in the first place. And that debate continued right up until the RFDS plane landed and a hold was put on proceedings while a ute was sent out to pick up the doctor and the nurse.

It was during this brief respite that Ziggie took on the responsibility of making a bush stretcher. The reasoning behind that was to save precious time so the blow-in could be placed into the back of the ute as soon as the doctor had checked him over. Ziggie slung a bit of canvas around a couple of bits of gidgee then rolled the unconscious blow-in onto the stretcher.

When the doctor arrived he went through the full medical procedure. 'This bloke's in an extremely critical condition,' he concluded. 'So fellers, when you pick up the stretcher, take it nice and easy.'

Now, constructing a house out of railway sleepers may have been one of Ziggie's fortes but making a bush stretcher out of a strip of canvas and a couple of bits of gidgee apparently wasn't. Because, when they lifted the stretcher, the canvas gave way and the blow-in fell straight through and hit his head on the railway track with an almighty thud.

'Holy Jesus,' someone said, 'we've killed him fer sure.'

But almost before those words had been spoken, the blow-in miraculously snapped back into consciousness. What's more, to everyone's surprise, particularly the doctor's, he sat bolt upright. He took one look at the menagerie of faces gawking down at him, then he had a quick glance out at the endlessly rolling red sandhills.

'Where the bloody hell am I?' he squawked.

'Barton,' came the reply, at which the blow-in got up, shook his head and staggered off down the track, leaving the doctor mystified and the locals only more reassured as to the weirdness of mankind in the outside world.

Of course, that included Ziggie and his seven dogs who wandered back home to tuck into a nice hearty breakfast.

Straight through Square Leg, by the Back Door, down the Side Path, out the Gate, over the Street and into the Pub

(Swampy)

The driveway is still there. Even now, thirty-five years on, it still looks very long, about a cricket pitch-and-a-half from the wrought-iron front gate to the garage door. The first half of the driveway is extremely narrow. It's bordered to the left by the brick wall of the shop, and to the right by a wooden and wire-meshed fence. The fence holds back a small leafy garden with a fig tree at its centre. Beyond the first fifteen metres, the driveway opens onto a larger grassed area.

That's where us kids played cricket.

The corrugated fence leading on from the end of the shop's brick wall to the garage protected the entire off-side of the field. The garage acted as the wicketkeeper and slips cordon. Fielding at short midwicket was a domed concrete well, a metre in height. If you clobbered one over the well, the louvred sleepout came into play. That spelt disaster. In the three years before I left Beckom to go to boarding school, Dad requisitioned more louvres from the stores department at head office than did all the other country branches combined. At deep fine leg, behind the garage, was the wood heap. A tall slatted fence covered the area from the wood heap around to backward square leg. The foreboding galah's cage stood at forward square leg. Peter, its occupant, was always the most vocal of spectators. 'Have a go ya mug!' he'd squawk at the most inconvenient times.

The only bountiful runs to be scored through this tightly packed field were from a well-timed hook. If you caught a bouncer just right, the ball flew between the galah's cage and the slatted fence and scooted straight through square leg, by the back door, down the side path, out the gate, over the street, and into the pub.

Whenever Dad joined in to give us some coaching, it was a standing offer that, if the ball went through the front door of the pub, he'd give the batsman a zack, as sixpence was called. It only happened twice. On both occasions Dad disappeared into the pub for what seemed like ages. At the time us kids stood around wondering why a cricket ball was so hard to find in such a small front bar.

But as I look down that long driveway now, cricket is the furthermost thing from my mind. I can almost feel Dad's presence here. He is close.

The bank — this bank in particular — was the mainstay of Dad's life for just on eight years. It shaped the way he thought, the way he acted, his high values of truth and honesty. As his only son those values were projected onto me, but in an odd sort of way. Dad was a great stickler for things like always being on time, wearing clean, shiny shoes, showing respect for your elders, having neatly groomed hair, being courteous to others, walking tall — chest out, shoulders back — and of course, swearing of any kind was strictly forbidden. So as I approached my sixteenth birthday, I was ever mindful of these things, especially when Dad was around.

Also, at that time, other things began to preoccupy my life, namely females. As I'd learned from bitter experience, the chances of a girl accepting an offer of a date, and the ultimate success of that date, related directly to whether or not you had a driver's licence and a car to drive.

For some reason Dad wasn't too keen on me getting a licence when I reached the legal age. Perhaps he might've known my sordid ulterior motives. Perhaps he was worried about his car. It surely didn't have anything to do with a lack of ability on my part, because I'd been driving utes and tractors at Yanco Ag. I harped and harped until, one Friday during school holidays, Dad broke his resolve and we drove down to the police station at Ardlethan to get a set of learner's plates.

After breakfast the following morning, Mum made Dad and me a packed lunch and we headed out over the Mirrool Creek to roam the dirt roads for driving lessons. As was usual with Dad, his plan was to teach me everything there was to know about driving in one day. As was usual with me, I expected it to take only half a day. And oddly enough, that's the way it happened. Dad was surprised how I seemed to have the knack of being able to synchronise the workings of the clutch and the gears while still maintaining course and control. After a couple of minor hiccups, even reverse parking seemed to fall into place.

Throughout the lesson, Dad peppered me with questions. There again, I got the vast majority of them right. So eager was I to get my licence that I'd stayed up most of the night studying the driver's manual.

'If only you had the same enthusiasm for your school work,' Dad uttered.

So it was with an overall air of accomplishment that we headed home that afternoon. Dad even promised to organise the driving test the following Monday.

As I drove back down the main street towards home, Dad asked if I'd be all right negotiating the narrow driveway, leading to the garage.

'A piece of cake,' I replied.

As I rounded the corner to line up the gates, it suddenly struck me just how small the margin for error was. And the closer we bore down on the gates, the more impossible it seemed that a car could fit through. Panic set in. My mind went blank. A full day of lessons flew out the window. I forgot where the clutch was. I forgot where the gears were. I forgot where the brake was. I forgot where the steering wheel was. The only thing I didn't seem to forget was the accelerator, because that's what I slammed my foot down on. Boy, did that old Holden have some power. It spun its wheels, the rear end slung around, and we just took off in a cloud of burning rubber. It was a complete miracle how that car managed to find its way through the gate — a miracle I didn't witness because my eyes were shut. When I opened them, to my left was the blur of the shop's brick wall. To my right was the blur of the fence. Ahead was the rapidly advancing garage door. Beside me, Dad was clinging onto the dashboard. His eyes were protruding from their sockets. His glasses were standing out from his face. His false teeth were clattering ten to the dozen.

'HOLY FUCKIN' JESUS CHRIST!' Dad screamed at the top of his voice.

That shocked me into action.

Amid the screeching of brakes and the crunching of gears, and with a slice of good luck, we shuddered to a halt within a whisker of the garage door.

Dad was out of that car in an instant. He leapt over the bonnet. And like a well-timed hook, he shot straight through square leg, by the back door, down the side path, out the gate, over the street and into the pub.

Quick

(Great Australian Shearing Stories)

There was this bloke, Albie, an Aboriginal feller he was, who used to be a shearer up around Perenjori, just south-east of Geraldton. Anyhow, people had a lot of respect for Albie, they did. If there was any trouble they'd come and get him and he'd go and step in and get things under control a bit. That's why he was regarded as 'The Black Prince' in Perenjori, because he used to keep the other fellers in line. Albie, his name was.

But this Albie was also a pretty good shearer. Bloody quick. And, what's more, he never missed the chance to remind people just how quick he was, because he was a pretty good storyteller as well.

He often told us the one about the time he was out shearing, and on this particular day he was really going for them; shearing away like crazy. Anyway, he was going down the whipping side of this sheep, clearly hammering away he was, and he mistakenly shore its leg clean off; shore the sheep's leg clean off, he did. So he said, 'Oh, Christ.' Then as quick as a flash he grabbed this needle and cotton, stuck the leg back on the sheep, and sewed it back on again. Now Albie said that the operation was over in a flash, so quick in fact that the sheep was down the chute and back out into the yard long before it'd even realised that its leg had been cut off.

'Well, that's fixed that,' Albie said to himself. 'The cocky won't notice.'

But then he reckoned that around smoko he happened to look out the window and there was this sheep walking around with its leg around back-to-front.

'Oh, Christ,' he said.

Now what he'd done was that he'd sewed the leg of the sheep back on so quick that he hadn't even noticed that it was on around the wrong way. Neither had the sheep. That's what Albie said.

Then there's the one about the time he went down to Perth to see a contractor about getting a job shearing out on the stations. And I know that this one's true because I was in the office with him when it happened. Anyway, he was having this interview with a contractor and the contractor chap said, 'Can yer shear a hundred in a day, sonny?'

And Albie looked down and said to him, 'Oh Christ, mate,' he said, 'it just depends on how many times yer want 'em done.'

So that's how quick Albie was. And he reckoned that he was just as quick even after he gave away shearing. He reckoned that he never lost his edge, so to speak. And this'll give you some idea as to just how quick he was, even later in his life.

See, back in the 1960s they were opening up a lot of land in Western Australia and they dished out a conditional-purchase block to Albie. Anyhow, Albie told us that he was out there clearing his block one day and when it came time for lunch he went and sat underneath this currajong tree. So there he was, eating his sandwich or whatever, when he suddenly felt something close by. There was a presence, like; a very dangerous presence.

So Albie spun around and there was this big black venomous snake with its head coming at him at the speed of a whip, about to strike him, like. Now that gave Albie about two minuses of a split second to avoid getting bit. But Albie reckoned that he was so quick he rolled out of the way, just in the nick of time, which caused the snake to miss him by a fraction and mistakenly sink its fangs into the currajong tree.

And Albie told us, he said, 'You know, I would've definitely been dead today if I weren't so quick,' he said, 'because I went back to that currajong tree two weeks later and it was dying from snakebite because all the leaves had fallen offa it.'

That was Albie. The Black Prince, they called him, and I believe that on more than one occasion he shore over three hundred a day and that would've been quite a few years back, probably back in the 1950s, I'd reckon. But, by the living Harry, he was quick.

One Day while Counting Sheep

(Great Australian Droving Stories)

I used to be in the navy many years ago. Anyway, we were steaming up the coast one time and, with nothing better to do, we were sitting up in the quarterdeck, bullshitting away to each other. This would've been in '59 or thereabouts.

Anyway, there was this bloke with us whose surname was Poor, so obviously we'd nicknamed him 'Pissy', as in Piss Poor. Pissy hailed from right out the back blocks of western New South Wales, and every mid-year leave and Christmas leave he used to go home, up the bush.So he came back from leave this time and, like I said, there we were spinning bullshit in the quarterdeck and Pissy told us this droving story about the largest mob of sheep he'd ever seen. And what's more, he swore that it was true. And knowing Pissy ... Well, you can make up your own mind.

Now when Pissy spoke, he talked in a real slow, laconic manner, so you've gotta imagine that, and you've also gotta imagine that Pissy's brother, having never been out of the bush in his life, talked even slower.

Anyway, Pissy and his brother were having a quiet beer or two, out on the front verandah of the pub, near where they lived.It was about ten o'clock in the morning, and they were sitting there, when this mob of sheep began meandering down the main street, past the pub, heading on their way out of town to wherever they were going.Then once each hour or so, a half-starved, flea bitten looking kelpie would happen to drift by, walking more with the mob than keeping them in any tight sheepdog order.

So with not too much else going on in town at the time, the two brothers grabbed another beer and they sat down again to watch this passing parade.Then a couple of hours later this mob of sheep was still wandering down the main street, past the pub, heading on their way out of town to wherever they were going.

By this time Pissy and his brother had had a few more beers and they were feeling a bit peckish so they decided to go inside the pub to have a counter lunch. And it was while they were having lunch that Pissy happened to remark to his brother, That's a fairly big mob'a sheep goin' past, aye?' To which the brother gave the statement a lot of thought while he ate another chop and had another beer.

'Reckon yer might be right,' the brother eventually replied.

Anyhow, after lunch they grabbed another beer and they went back out on the verandah only to find this mob of sheep was still coming down the main street, past the pub, heading on their way out of town to wherever they were going. So with nothing better to do they took up their seats again to watch some more sheep drift by. And like I said, once each hour or so a half-starved, flea bitten looking kelpie would aimlessly wander past with the mob. Now why Pissy made a point of mentioning about the dog was because it was something that his brother was to suddenly remark on.

There goes another dog,' Pissy's brother said, seemingly fascinated by how the occasional, half-starved dog broke the monotony of colour; the dogs being brownish and the sheep being a dirty white-grey-reddish colour.

Anyway, they had a few more beers and at about four o'clock in the afternoon they were still there, watching this mob coming down the main street, past the pub, heading on their way out of town.

So Pissy and his brother had a few more beers and it was just coming on sunset when a horse and sulky appeared in the distance. Now, mind you, this sulky wasn't bringing up the rear of the mob because it still looked like there were thousands of sheep coming up along behind it.

So they waited a while longer and had a few more beers and, when the bloke with the horse and sulky finally got close enough, Pissy and his brother noticed that the sulky was loaded to the hilt with pots and pans and cooking gear of all shapes and sizes. Loaded to overflowing it was, with all this cooking gear.

'I reckon that bloke's the camp cook,' Pissy said to his brother, to which his brother contemplated the statement while he finished off his beer, lifted his hat, and scratched his head.

'Reckon yer might be right,' he said.

Now, by this stage, this almost ten-hour parade of sheep had started to get to Pissy's brother, and his highly inquisitive brain began a complex mathematical process of trying to work out just how many bloody sheep there were in this mob. So when the cook got near enough to the pub, Pissy's brother grabbed his beer and wandered through the sheep and over to the sulky, which, as I said, was loaded to the hilt with pots and pans and cooking gear of all shapes and sizes.

'Mate,' he said to the cook, 'just how many head'a sheep do yer reckon yer got?'

'Buggered if I know,' the bloke replied. 'I just cook fer the bloody dogs 'n' I've lost count'a them.'

As Full as a Boot

(The Complete Book of Australian Flying Doctor Stories)

No doubt you've heard of the term 'as full as a boot'. Well, here's a story that'll take some beating. It's about a Padre who went one better.

It happened back in the Christmas of 1937 when, after a stint of work on a station up in the middle of Cape York, a stockman, a real gentlemanly cove he was, came down to Normanton to celebrate. Now this type of celebration was, and still is, a bush ritual. After a group of stockmen have been out living and working in cattle camps for months on end, as soon as the mustering season is over they take a break and head straight for civilisation, and in particular to the nearest watering hole, there to celebrate.

Anyway, along with his mates, this chap arrived at the National Hotel in Normanton determined to enjoy himself. And as occasionally happens in these situations, he got a bit carried away. Well, more than just a bit, really. He overcelebrated to such an extent that when he decided to go to bed, he encountered great difficulty in climbing the two flights of stairs leading to his second-storey room. But patience is a virtue and he awkwardly edged his way upwards, step by precarious step, much to the admiration and encouragement of his mates.

Given the condition this feller was in, he did a sterling job. That is until he was about to take the final step in that almost 'Hillarian' climb to the summit. As he turned to wave to the cheering crowd below, a minor mishap of judgment occurred and, lo and behold, back down the stairs he came, thump ...

thump ... thump, until he reached the bottom and there he stayed, unconscious and injured.

After the unfortunate accident, the publican got in touch with the Australian Inland Mission at Cloncurry — the AIM being the organisation that pioneered the Royal Flying Doctor Service — saying that the chap was in real trouble at the foot of the stairs.

'Looks like the poor bloke's injured his noggin and broke his shoulder bone,' the publican explained.

Now this was the first real 'Flying Doctor' trip that the particular Padre in question had gone out on. Normally he was a patrol parson with the Presbyterian Church who, in turn, ran the Australian Inland Mission. And it was his job to cover the area from Birdsville to Normanton and beyond by road, that's if you could describe some of the bush tracks that he travelled over as being roads. In actual fact, he virtually lived in his truck, covering hundreds of miles each year, christening bush children, installing pedal wireless sets, and so forth. John Flynn used to travel with him quite a bit.

Anyway, as this clergyman prepared to get on the plane, the doctor picked up on his apprehension.

'Padre,' the doctor said, 'don't worry. This is just a plain evacuation. We'll go out there, collect this feller, and bring him straight back to Cloncurry. All will be hunky-dory.'

With those words of assurance, they clambered into the small Fox Moth 83 Ambulance aeroplane. After turning the propeller, the pilot jumped into the outside cockpit and prepared for take-off.

Now the Fox Moth 83 was by no means an aeroplane designed for passenger comfort. It only had enough room for two seats, a stretcher and the doctor. What's more, it was held together with little more than wood, cloth, string and wire. So they set off at top speed, which was about 80 miles an hour, in the old money; about a four-hour trip it was.

When they arrived in Normanton they headed straight for the National Hotel, fully expecting to find this chap still laying at the bottom of the stairs. But nothing was going to get in the way of this stockman's big occasion. This was his big night. It was his ritual and nothing was going to curtail his celebrations, not even head injuries, nor concussion, nor shoulder injuries. Nothing! Somehow he'd gained his second wind and had managed to find his way back to the bar.

Now this chap proved to be a big man of around 15 stone, if not more. Quite a 'bush gentleman' he was, in his own sort of way, and one who could tell cattle-camp yarns by the dozen, which he seemed more intent on doing at the time than returning to Cloncurry to get his injuries seen to. But in the end four mates got him into a truck and they drove him out to the airstrip.

But getting this chap out there was only part of the fun. Like I said, he was a solid lump of a man and it took some wangling to get him into the Fox Moth and fixed up in one of the seats in the cabin. When that was done, the doctor clambered in, followed by the clergyman who sat beside the stockman. The pilot spun the propeller, the plane sparked into action, then he jumped into the outside cockpit and they prepared for take-off.

'Just keep an eye on the patient, Padre,' the doctor said, and they took off, heading back to Cloncurry.

As I said, it was a good four-hour trip, longer when there's an extra 15 stone on board. There they were, halfway to Cloncurry, and they were flying over Donor's Hill when the big stockman made it known that he'd received the urgent call of nature. His exact words won't be quoted. All I'll say is that the stockman used his own particular style of vernacular to get his point across in a crystal clear manner. The rest is up to your own imagination.

Naturally, the Fox Moth 83 didn't have the facilities to cater for such an exotic exercise. But that wasn't going to inhibit the stockman. As enterprising as he was, he took off one of his riding boots. Out it come, and he proceeded to fill the boot. Then after the stockman had filled the boot, he stood it up on the floor next to the Padre. Now if that didn't give our good clergyman a shock, worse was to follow. The stockman then removed the other boot, the left one it might have been, and proceeded to fill that one up as well, or nearly up.

'Ah, there, that's better,' he sighed and calmly stood it up beside the other one, right next to the Padre's seat.

So there was the Padre, watching these two boots jiggle precariously about on the floor of the vibrating aeroplane, when the voice of the pilot crackled through the speaking tube from the outside cockpit. 'Hold on tight, fellers,' he said, 'we're going to strike some rough turbulence over these Cloncurry hills.'

That really threw the Padre into panic. He took a look at the stockman. Then he took a look at the jiggling boots. Then he took a second look at the stockman. But the stockman didn't seem too perturbed about the matter so the clergyman was forced to take things into his own hands, so to speak, and as they flew through the turbulence over the Cloncurry hills, he steadied both boots to keep them from spilling all over the place.

They finally landed in Cloncurry where the ambulance was waiting. As soon as they came to a stop, four husky men helped lift the bulky, injured patient out of the plane and into the ambulance.

'See you later, Padre,' the doctor said as he jumped in the back of the ambulance, and off they dashed to the hospital, leaving the Padre behind.

So there he was, this Padre, standing out on the airstrip, wondering how he was going to get home when it suddenly dawned upon him that he was still hanging on to these two filled stockman's boots.

He must have looked a rare sight because the pilot appeared not long after, and didn't he have a chuckle. 'Well,' he laughed, 'I've heard of the saying "as full as a boot"—but, Padre, I reckon you might have gone one better there!'

Sammy and Chocko

(Great Australian Shearing Stories)

There was this shearer guy, who shall remain completely nameless, except that I'll call him 'Sammy' for the sake of the story. And this Sammy had a constant companion, his shadow really, and that was a little curly French terrier called Chocko. I can still remember the name, Chocko.

Anyway, Sammy never talked directly to nobody, not that I ever saw at least. Like, when he wanted a few more sheep penned up, he wouldn't look over at you and ask you to pen some more sheep up. He'd never do that. What he'd do was to give you the message via Chocko and you were supposed to overhear it. Like he'd say, 'Chocko, you'd better tell that young feller to pen a few more sheep up.'

Sammy never spoke directly to no one, always through his dog, Chocko. So that was Sammy, and that was his dog, Chocko.

So Sammy and the others were crutching with some other fellers one time and at morning tea, morning smoko, they'd down their handpieces and head over to the shearers' quarters for their break. That's where I also happened to be living. In the shearers' quarters.

Now, it soon became more than a little bleeding obvious that Sammy liked his bit of home-brewed port, see. Well, Sammy called it port, anyway. He'd say with reference to me, 'Ah Chocko,' he'd say to the dog, 'that young feller likes a bit a port, do yer reckon that he might like a taste?'

So I did. I had a mouthful. But only that once because by the heck it had a kick. It almost booted the roof of me mouth open it did. So that was enough for me, just the one swig.

Anyway, this particular time it was a stinking hot morning and the temperature had risen rapidly through the thirties by smoko then up into the forties by lunch, and still the mercury continued rising. So Sammy was crutching away with Chocko laying close by, panting with the heat, when at about two o'clock there came this terrific chain of explosions from out behind the shed, see.

Now Sammy drove a model T Ford, which he had parked out the back, which was where the explosions had come from. Now the old Ford used to have a big boot lid, you see, a 'dickey' boot it was called. So if you opened the boot lid back it exposed two more seats, giving you room to carry a couple more passengers. But in Sammy's case it gave him the extra room he needed to transport all his flagons of grog around.

So anyway, we rushed out the back of the shed to see that Sammy's dickey boot had been blown completely open. What's more, there was a mass of foam flowing out and broken glass was bloody everywhere.

Now what had happened was that the extreme heat had caused the first flagon of Sammy's home-brewed port to explode, which had set off a chain reaction, taking out a second flagon, which had taken out a third, then the fourth until eventually about eight flagons of the stuff had gone up, *Oomph!*

Anyhow, I'll never forget the scene. Sammy's trousers used to join at the knees. There was a reason for that. The crutch hung down around his knees so that he could prop the sheep up in the sort of cradle it made between his legs. But I can still remember Sammy looking at the demolished dickey boot of his model T Ford with his ever-faithful Chocko at his side. There they were, they both stood like stunned mullets there for a while. Then finally Sammy pushed his hat back on his head with his index finger.

'Well Chocko,' he said, 'I knew that home brew were pretty strong bloody stuff but I didn't reckon she were that bloody potent.'

Unscratchable

(Great Australian Railway Stories)

Basically, my story starts with my grandfather. It's a bit hazy, but I know he worked on the construction of the narrow gauge from Peterborough, across the Willochra Plain, to Quorn, in the 1920s, and in about 1936 he worked on the construction of the Port Augusta to Port Pirie line. Then my dad started with the railways in 1936 and ended up as a loco superintendent before retiring in 1978. So between the three of us, we've clocked up well over 100 years with the railways.

But Dad was very well known and he had quite a few 'firsts'. Like, in about 1974, he took the first Indian Pacific to Western Australia. He was also the first to drive the standard gauge Ghan to Marree. He also drove the first Bud Diesel Car out of South Australia. The Bud was a 'passenger' with a similar configuration to the Adelaide metro-trains. He also drove the last steam engine from Port Augusta to Quorn. Unfortunately, he died the October before last but, as a young feller, I used to travel with him on the steam engines to Alice Springs. That was a remarkable experience because those were very different times and I used to travel on the engine with him, which was absolutely illegal. But one of my favourite memories of being with Dad was on one trip when we were coming back from Alice Springs.

It was around 1954, I'd reckon. Dad was driving the goods down from Alice Springs and we got to a place called Beltana on Christmas Eve. Of course, the crew were all disappointed that they wouldn't be home with their families for Christmas. So, in an attempt to make the most of it, Dad and his fireman went across to the hotel at Beltana to ask the publican, an old chap by the name of Ted Nichols, if he'd put on a bit of a Christmas dinner for us all the next day. Ted was pretty receptive to all that. 'Yep,' he said, 'I'll do that for yer but I'd like a little job done in return.'

Naturally, my father and his fireman said, 'Yeah, that's fine. What do yer want?'

'Oh,' Ted said, 'I need some help to shift a refrigerator.'

In those days the refrigerators were kerosene fridges and they were very, very heavy. Now, poor old Ted had a few physical problems, one of which was he had a glass eye, and another was that he had a wooden leg. Being only very young I wasn't much help, so I was just standing there watching the three of them staggering around with this fridge. But when they got to the doorway they struck trouble because the door wasn't very wide. So, there they were, trying to get this damn fridge through the door when, next thing, poor old Ted's glass eye popped out. Then as he bent over to pick up his eye, his wooden leg fell off. Now, I was absolutely stunned by all this but Dad's fireman, as quick as a flash, said, 'By Jesus, Ted,' he said, 'I've never seen a man fall to pieces so quick under pressure.'

So that's one thing that happened when I was with Dad. Anyway, when they closed the old Ghan line in 1955, approximately half the railway personnel from Quorn were transferred to Alice Springs and half went to Stirling North, about eight miles from Port Augusta. So in 1959 I started in the Commonwealth Railway's Stores at Stirling North as a 'spud boy'. The job was called a spud boy simply because that's what I did. The spuds would arrive in big hessian bags and I'd put them into smaller bags for retail purposes. I did other things, too, of course. But I was there for about nine months until I passed my entrance exam and joined the railways as an apprentice boilermaker. Then I stayed in the area of the workshops for about ten years before going out on the Nullarbor Plain, doing the fairly unique job of the continuous welding of the railway line. But that's another story.

Now, it might seem like I have some sort of fetish for glass eyes but, while I was in the workshops, this young feller — a real card — well, he had a glass eye. The history there was that his mother had contracted measles when she was pregnant and, as a result, this chap'd been born with only one eye. Then after some years he was fitted with a glass one.

At that stage, I'd just been appointed as an angle-ironsmith. That trade's gone now but, simply, it involved the making or manufacturing of the different forms of steel that weren't produced as a standard by BHP. See, we had steam engines still running around that'd been built back in 1922 and, of course, a lot of the components for those weren't made anymore, so it was my job to make them. The immediate area I worked in had a coke oven and also there was a very big cast-iron block. Now, this block was roughly eight foot square by about two foot thick. It probably weighed six or seven ton and it had a machined flat surface that I could bang away on to form this steel. Anyway, I was standing alongside this block one day and the chap with the glass eye come up, so I said, 'How are yer going?'

'Pretty good,' he said. 'I just got a new eye.'

'Oh,' I said, 'have yer?'

He said, 'Yeah.' And he had this habit of just ripping his glass eye out of its socket to show everybody. So he ripped it out. 'Look,' he said, 'what do yer think of that? It's unscratchable.'

Of course, I said, 'Don't be stupid. Nothing's unscratchable.' I said, 'Look, a diamond's one of the hardest things known to mankind and you can scratch that, so there's no way known that your new glass eye is unscratchable.'

'Bullshit,' he said. 'It's unscratchable.'

With that he got this glass eye of his and he threw it down, hard on the steel block. Well, if you can imagine throwing a golf ball or a marble down onto a steel block, well, this eye simply rebounded off the block and it shot straight up in the air. Now, like many workshops of the day, the roof was angled like the teeth of a saw. At its highest it was 59 feet. Anyway, up goes this eye and, of course, he's running around with his hands held out, ready to catch it when it comes down. But it doesn't come down, see.

'I've lost me eye,' this feller said.

'I'll get it,' I said. And so I went to the 60 ton overhead crane driver and I asked him if he'd drive me up and down the workshop on his crane to see if I could find this glass eye, up in the roof.

'Okay,' he said.

So this driver took me along until, sure enough, in one of the gables up in the rafters here's this eye looking at me. It was a bit hairy but I climbed up the edge of the crane and onto the rafters and picked the eye up out of all the dust and crap. Then I took the eye back down and gave it back to the bloke who'd lost it.

'Thanks,' he said, and without even wiping it, he just stuck it straight back in his eye socket. But then he must've thought about it because he popped it back out again and he showed me.

'See, have a look,' he said. 'I told you it was unscratchable.'

And so help me God, there wasn't a mark on it.

Noccundra — Qld

(Great Australian Stories: Outback Towns and Pubs)

Considering how the infamous horse thief cum dubious-explorer cum dodgy character Andrew Hume — no relation to Hamilton Hume of Hume and Hovell fame — died of thirst out this way, while he was searching for the missing Ludwig Leichhardt expedition, it's no small wonder that the first building to be erected at Noccundra was the pub. That was in 1882 and it remains the town's only occupied building. And even to this very day, thirst prevention remains an extremely high priority for the few locals and for the tourists that visit the place.

Now, for those that don't know, Noccundra's in the southwestern corner of Queensland, in the Cooper Creek–Wilson River area and the story goes that we were flying out to Tibooburra to do a RFDS clinic when we received an urgent request to divert to Noccundra. Someone had been severely burnt. The odd thing was, though, the chap who put through the call couldn't stop laughing. Naturally we thought it mustn't have been too serious, and we said so. But the chap, the one who was laughing, was adamant that the victim was badly burnt, and yes, it was anything but a laughing matter, which he was, if that makes any sense.

Now, as the story unfolded, it'd been a stifling hot, still day and a few of the locals had gravitated to the Noccundra pub attempting to prevent a thirst. The problem being that a large tiger snake was thinking along the same lines. It appeared in the pub, had a look around, but when it saw the accumulated gathering, it decided that it didn't like the company and so it headed off to the next best place it could think of, that being the outside toilet — one of those long-drop types. So out of the pub the tiger snake slithered, down the track a bit, into the outside toilet, and it disappeared down the long-drop, where it was nice and cool.

I'd better not mention any names so, for the sake of the story, we'll call the chap Joe. Now, Joe saw where the snake had gone and he came up with the bright idea of incinerating it. He downed his drink, put on his hat, went and siphoned a gallon of petrol out of his ute, then wandered back through the pub, down the track a bit, into the outside toilet, and he tossed the fuel down the long-drop, where the snake was. The problem being, after he tossed the petrol down the long-drop, he searched through his pockets and couldn't find his matches.

So he wandered back inside the pub. 'Anyone seen me matches?' he asked.

As I said, it was a very hot, still day. Stinking hot, in fact. So after Joe found his matches, he thought that he may as well have another thirst quencher before he went back outside and sorted out the snake. Meantime the petrol fumes were rising up from out of the long-drop and, with there not being a breath of a breeze to disperse them, the toilet soon become nothing short of a pending, gigantic powder keg.

Anyhow, after Joe had downed his drink, he grabbed his matches and put his hat back on. 'I'll be back in a tick,' he said, then he wandered outside, down the track a bit, in the direction of the toilet and, without having a clue as to what he was in for, he walked into the toilet and took out his matches.

'Goodbye, snake,' he said and struck a match over the longdrop.

Now, there are those from the outlying districts that go so far as to say that they felt the reverberations of the ensuing explosion. I don't know so much about that but one thing's for sure, it certainly put the wind up the blokes in the bar of the Noccundra pub. Such was the instantaneous impact of the blast that they didn't even have the time to down their drinks before they hit the floor. Mind you, that's only a rumour because knowing some of the chaps out that way, no matter what the emergency, they'd always finish their drinks before taking any action, even if it is a reflex action.

Still, you've got to feel sorry for poor old Joe. Left standing over what'd once been the Noccundra pub's long-drop toilet, his clothes smouldering away. Critically burnt he was and he stunk to high-heaven as well. And the shock, poor bloke. Even by the time we arrived he was still standing there, as dazed as a stunned mullet.

Turkey

(Great Australian Railway Stories)

Even though this happened back in 1951, I still won't mention names or places as I may incriminate the innocent and the guilty, of which I may or may not have been one of either of those two parties. But tell me if you've heard it before because a few of these things that went on some time ago have been so much spoken about that they've become wide knowledge. Still, this one's based on actual facts even though I might or might not have been there at the time, like I said. Anyhow, there was this particular train crew that worked out along a small bush branch line and once every week they'd take the old steamer out to deliver and pick up a few goods, plus the occasional passenger, on their way to the end of the line and back. Now, in a pretty isolated spot along this line was situated a turkey farm and throughout the year this train crew had sussed out this mob of turkeys and they were looking delicious. So by the time they'd started out on their last trip before Christmas they'd decided to swipe one of these turkeys for their Christmas dinner.

Of course, being good mates, the whole crew was in on it, including the guard. So on their way out they pulled up beside this turkey farm. As usual there was no-one about so the fireman hops off with his wheat bag at the ready, he jumps the fence and he grabs one of these turkeys, a nice big plump one. All goes exactly to plan so he jumps back on the train and off they go again with this turkey all wrapped up in the wheat bag, pending Christmas dinner. Now, unbeknown to the train crew, the farmer saw all this happen. So he gets in touch with the cops, explains what he saw, and tells them to meet him at the station at the end of the line. 'Be prepared to make arrests,' the farmer tells the sergeant of police.

Well, just before you get to the station at the end of the line there's this big, walloping, long, sweeping bend. So the train starts to come around this huge bend and the ever-alert fireman sees, in the distance, all these BSA motorbikes lined up on the platform. And the closer they get to the station the more he and the train driver come to realise that these motorbikes belonged to the police. 'What're we gonna do?' said the fireman to the driver. To which the driver took a look at the wheat bag containing the nicked turkey followed by a look towards the firebox. 'Ditch the evidence,' he replied with a tear coming to his eye.

So the fireman grabs the wheat bag and into the firebox it goes. 'Goodbye, Christmas,' he says, and up goes the turkey in a puff of smoke.

Anyhow, when they pull into the station the farmer and the police come aboard and say, 'Alright, where is it?'

'Where's what?' the driver and fireman say.

'The turkey,' the police say.

'We don't know anything about a turkey,' came the reply.

So the police, along with the farmer, search the cab of the train. No turkey there. Then they go digging around in the coal on the tender. No turkey there. So they go through the couple of carriages.

Still no turkey. Then they get to the guard's van. 'Have you seen the turkey?' they question the guard.

'What turkey?' he says.

So they scour through the guard's van. Still no turkey.

'Look,' said the driver, 'we're running late and we never run late.' Which was a complete load of bull but with that, the guard blows his whistle and the driver starts moving the train out of the station, leaving the cops to leap back onto the platform, there to try and explain to the farmer how they can't arrest anyone without the evidence being produced.

Anyhow, as it turned out the fireman, who was a pretty clever chap, had brought along an extra wheat bag, just in case. And with knowing that the farmer was still back at the railway station debating the pros and cons of the law with the police, he said to the driver, 'How's about we grab another one on the way back?'

So they did and, yes, I do remember that particular Christmas very well. In fact, it turned out to be one of my most enjoyable Christmases in my many, many years as a fireman on the railways.

Salted Meat and Damper

(Great Australian Droving Stories)

I've got a thick skin so I don't mind if you use my name. It's John Davies and I was born in 1931, which makes me seventy-one this year. Luckily though, I'm in good health because I could've been dead yesterday, and there's plenty of my old mates who've died, and a lot younger than me.

Anyway, I started off breaking in horses when I was very young. But I got a bit jack of that so I picked up with some one-horse drovers around Warren, in western New South Wales. Then I picked up with some other fellers and we went out west, between Coolabah and Byrock, to a station at Glenariff Siding, halfway between Nyngan and Bourke. So I was there for three and half years, maybe four, doing droving and stock work. That was in 1948, when I was seventeen.

I also did some droving for a feller, Jackie Malloy, from Forbes. He was a ex-rodeo rider. Now I never wanted to try my living at buck-jumping but I was a good hand with animals and we also used to educate a lot of horses for station owners. They'd have a toey horse, something a bit snorty and lively, and they'd say, 'Look, take him with yer fer a while then bring him back when yer've fixed him.'

Of course, if the horse was any good you lost him, sort of, and he never went back. Same with the dogs. We'd get a lot of dogs to work and if they turned out any good, well, we'd sort of lose them too. It wasn't dishonesty. It's just that the good ones seemed to wander, somehow. Strange that, aye.

Anyhow, from there I went up to Birdsville and on to the Diamantina. See, it was a great dream for us horsey blokes to go into the Channel Country. It was the pick of Queensland in those days. You could fatten bullocks there like nothing. Unbelievable.

But it was all horse work. That's what got me. I would not have stayed anywhere without horses and stock. And it was all outside; open camps, working out in the bush. I mean, in those days, if we got into town once every three months we were laughing, really laughing. But you didn't give a bugger. We loved the work. We wanted it. We loved the horses, and the money was completely bloody unimportant because, when you went droving, all you got was one pound a day, plus keep. This was in '47, maybe '48. And you never got paid while you were going out with the boss drover. You only got paid from the time he took delivery of the cattle, up until they were delivered. That's all. No travel, out and back.

Then at times, the cooks were very flighty. Out on the stations they went into dispute very quick. You could have a cook for two or three months or you might only have him for a day or two before he cleared off. They were like that. I mean, all those stories you hear about crooked, drunken, and cantankerous cooks are pretty true.

There was one cook — only a little feller, just like me. And see, you'd come in and you'd pick your meal up off the counter, then you'd go and sit down to eat. Anyhow, this cook used to serve up some very bloody ordinary meals. And of a night-time he'd always put out custard for sweets. That's all, just bloody custard.

So there's eight or ten of us there one night and I said, 'Can't yer serve anything else other than bloody custard, or at least put something in the stuff to give it some taste?'

Well, didn't he have a snap at me.

Then the next night, up comes this bloody custard again, so I had another go at him. 'Can't yer cook anything else?' I said.

By this time, I'd sat down. Anyhow, this cook, he grabbed a big boning knife and he came flying around the table, straight at me. But instead of stabbing me, he flicked the knife in the bowl and out came this piddly bloody apricot. I mean, the animal had gone and stuck this half apricot in the bottom of the bowl and then he'd smothered it with custard. Of course, I hadn't seen the bloody thing. Neither had anybody else. But holy shit, the whole lot of us were out through that bloody door in a shot. I tell you, nobody had any sweets that night. We disappeared.

But with the droving, I did a lot of the cooking myself. And cooking in a drover's camp's hard bloody work. It's a hell of a job. See, depending on how many men you had, you'd kill a beast every week or so. That's because you'd only be able to keep fresh meat for a couple of days before it went off, then you salted as much as you could.

See what happened was, you shot and bled him. Then you'd skin from a bit over halfway down the backbone to the gut, across the front and back legs, then you'd peel the hide back. Now because you only had two tucker packs to carry fresh meat, you'd keep a bit of the good steak and also some for stewing. Then you laid all the meat that you were going to salt, out on bushes — mulga or whatever — and you rubbed the salt into that and packed it away the next morning. But because bloody salted meat sweats some thing terrible, you had to lay it out again every night, to cool it; air it. I mean, this stuff's not like the corned meat you get at the butcher's. It's not like that at all.

Then at breakfast you had a bit of damper, because that's all there was. And sometimes you might have some of the leftover stew or curry from the night before, to go with the damper. That'd be done in the camp oven or bedourie. Anyway, you never ate much of a morning because you'd be up early getting your horses ready then, by piccaninny daylight, you'd leave camp.

But it was real damper. There wasn't bread in those days. That only came in later. Mind you, this was at the end of the war when things were still rationed. People don't realise that tea, sugar and clothes were rationed for a long time. I can still remember sending butter and clothing coupons to my mother and she'd send back tea coupons. Tea was scarce. You rarely had tea, so we drank coffee, and the coffee was horrible. You boiled it in a billy and, Holy Jesus, it was dreadful bloody stuff.

Then on the odd occasion we got macaroni and vermicelli. Oh God, when that happened, you'd think you were in bloody heaven. You'd cook it up with powdered milk and you'd put sugar on it. What a treat that was, I can tell you. But you never saw vegetables. I mean, they might throw in a pumpkin or a few potatoes when you first started out but, after those were gone, that was it. You never saw vegetables again. And there wasn't any canned stuff in those days. That only came later, in the '50s.

So basically we lived on salted meat and damper. And because of that, we used to get Barcoo rot. It's like scurvy and it's brought about because we ate no vitamins. See, how people lived later on, after the unions come in with all their rules about how you were supposed to live and what you were supposed to eat, well, there were no bloody rules like that when we were out there. If you didn't like it, you just got the bloody sack and you pissed off. That's all there was to it.

But jeez, it got cold. People think that just because you're travelling through a desert it gets hot. Well it might get hot in the summer but in winter it's bloody freezing. So much so that, in the morning, you had to let your camp sheet and swag thaw out before you could roll them up.

And we used those green-hide hobbles; peg hobbles, about a foot long and doubled over with a wooden peg through one end, and the other end had a slit in it where you pushed the peg through to lock it. I mean, they were soft enough of a night, when you put them on, but by morning they'd be frozen stiff. And also, you'd get back to camp and your hands were frozen, and if you put them near the fire they hurt bloody worse. Then if you put them in hot water, it hurt worse still. So it was a matter of belting them against your side until they thawed out.

But it was a magic life, so we didn't care. I mean, I wouldn't have given a stuff if me hands had fallen off because you just loved the work.

And also with the cold; see, most of our work was done around the sandhills, where you got big lumps of spinifex, so we'd throw a wax match into that and it'd flare up like crazy. And it didn't even frighten the horses. It was that bloody cold that they'd push in around the fire to warm themselves up, as well.

But with the food; because we ate so much salted meat and damper, we'd get constipated something terrible. Anyhow, with the constipation, you may remember that old saying about how you had to 'shift the bun'. Well fresh meat'd do that in a flash. See, on the nights you killed a beast, we all cooked our own meal. The cook didn't do anything. So if you wanted a bit of liver or kidney or the ribs or whatever, you just cut that off the beast and you cooked it yourself.

So after you had fresh meat that night, then again for breakfast, by jeez, you'd go gastric. And you'd feel it coming on and you'd get off your horse, and when the others saw you, they'd ride ahead and, of course, your horse'd want to follow them. So there you'd be, hanging onto the reins, struggling to go to the toilet, with your bloody pants down around your ankles and the bloody horses pulling away and you'd be shitting all over the sandhills.

And that's true. A while back, I put all that into the oral history at the National Museum in Canberra, and the feller from there asked me, 'How did you get on for toilets?'

There was no worries,' I said. 'We had 50,000 square miles of them.'

'But,' he asked, 'did you dig holes or anything?'

'Not really,' I said. 'We just went when we went.'

But you could always tell the boss drover because he'd have a roll of toilet paper in his bloody pack while the rest of us had nothing but a handful of spinifex. And I mean, have you ever felt that spinifex? It's dangerous stuff, I tell you.

A Shearer's Life

(Great Australian Shearing Stories)

Well mate, you could say that I've been shearing for far too long. That's how long I've been at it and I guess that I'll continue on with it for a while longer yet, as least as long as my body holds up. But no, I must admit that I'm well past the best of me years. Well past. And I know that I should've given the game away years ago. Me mate Ted'd even tell you that. A lot of people would. But I didn't and that's it. But that's just the way it is with shearing.

See, shearing gets in your blood. It's a way of life; a good way too, I reckon. I mean, you're out there, there's the freedom. You're with your mates. You don't have anything to worry about except the next sheep coming up the race so you just get stuck into it and do the job. Basically it's as simple as that, really. You take them as they come, one after the other.

Mind you, it's pretty hard work too. Don't get me wrong. It's very hard work. Bloody hard. But see, I started in the sheds when I was a youngster of around fourteen. And when it's all you've done since leaving school, you just don't know any different, do you? I mean, imagine a bloke like me working in some office in Perth, or a factory for instance, even in a bush town over here in WA. You couldn't, could you? It'd bloody well kill me.

But no, you get to meet some characters alright. There's the good and the bad there too but there's some real characters, I can tell you. See, I work the long run, have done for years, and the long run goes from up the north of Western Australia, right down to the south. So we cover some ground. We're away for around ten months at a time, see. I mean, we had a bloody cook one time. A big bastard he was too, and a fucking drunk to boot. Now, don't get me wrong, I drink, meself. I admit to that. I drink a lot, but this cook not only drunk a lot, he also drunk anything he could lay his bloody hands on. And what's more, he also ate all the good stuff then fed us the shit which was why the bastard was so fucking fat. I mean, this bloke didn't walk, he waddled. That's how big he was. He would've been at least twenty stone and that's at the least.

But, anyway, this cook feller got something like piles, or something like that it might've been, either that or a chafed arse because he was so fat and the cheeks of his bum used to rub together. Anyway, the upshot of it all was that he had some problem or other in the arse area between his cheeks. So he was talking to Ted one time and Ted told him that he knew a bloke once who had a similar sort of problem and what this feller had done was that he grabbed a handful of flour and he rubbed it up between the cheeks of his arse.

So that was that. Then that afternoon after work someone happened to look in the storeroom and they noticed that the bag of flour had these two huge bun marks on the top of it. Like, this bloody cook feller, instead of taking a handful of flour and rubbing it up between the cheeks of his arse, he just sat on top of the opened bag of flour and wiggled his buns into it. Christ almighty, can you imagine that! And to make matters worse, this cook feller was going to bake fresh bread for our tea, and we would've eaten the stuff.

Well, he didn't last long after that, I can tell you. We just about run him out of the shed. It didn't worry us how it'd take a week or so to get another cook up from Perth or wherever. He was gone like a shot. But the only trouble was that this drunken cook feller had gone and squatted in the only bag of flour we had and of course, bread's a staple part of a shearer's diet.

Then to make matters worse, the new cook forgot to bring up another bag of flour when he came up from Perth. So there we were, we were out in the middle of the donga and we're stuck with what we had. Just the one bag of flour with two huge bun marks in the top of it. So in the end we scraped off the top part of the flour, the part where the bastard had rubbed his arse in it, then we started using what was left. I mean, what else could we do?

But there were some pretty queer comments made about that, I can tell you, and some pretty sceptical blokes eating the bread. Real squirmy they were. Some of the fellers used to check it over a dozen or so times before they ate it. But no, the best thing to do was to just wolf it down and try not to think about it. That was the best thing to do.

But like I said, while shearing's been good for me, it's also had its other side. The bad side. Like, I've been married three times now, and divorced three times to boot. So I'm fifty-three and I'm on me Pat Malone at the moment. But, I mean, when you're away for most of the year it's hard to keep things together on the home front and that's because things change. So by the time you get back for Chistmas with the missus, well, she's gotten used to not having you around. And then you start getting on each other's goat and you end up having a barney or something, so you try and make it up to her by taking her out for a Chinese or something special. Maybe a night out at the dogs or the trots.

But no, that causes some real problems. I mean, after you've been away shearing with your mates for most of the year it's hard to get the knack of settling down with a woman again, even if it's only for a month or so.

Elliston — SA

(Great Australian Stories: Outback Towns and Pubs)

I'd say it would've been around the end of June 1972 that a mate and I went over to the west coast of South Australia to do a spot of fishing. Anyhow, we ended up at a beautiful little place on the Eyre Peninsula, called Elliston. From memory, I think the pub we stayed in was called the Elliston Hotel.

See, when we went to the bar, my mate kindly offered to buy me a glass of Grandfather Port. Now, up until that stage, I'd never had a taste of that particular port before and, mind you, I've never had a taste of it since. So we had this glass of Grandfather Port then, as what happens, we had a few more and at some stage of the evening we got talking to the publican.

'So yer like yer Grandfather Port, ay?' he said.

My mate said, 'Yes I do, very much. It's a bit expensive but it's a nice drop.'

Anyway, the publican says, 'Well, you and yer liking for Grandfather Port reminds me of an old story I was told, from many years ago.'

'Yeah,' we said.

And he told us a story that went something like this: see, premyxomatosis there was an old rabbiter who'd set up camp somewhere out of Elliston and he scraped out a meagre living by selling skins to the local dealer plus the occasional carcasses to the butcher and to some of the locals. Then, like so many did back in those days, this feller kept a shotgun close at hand, just in case he came upon a snake or got attacked by a dingo. Actually, rumour had it that, around Elliston at the time this story took place, there was a particularly vicious rogue dingo who'd been known to have, and I quote, 'ripped a few people to shreds' as the publican described it.

Anyhow, one day the old rabbiter had come into town to sell his skins and carcasses. Now, something I forgot was that the only transport this feller had was an old pushbike. That's all, an old pushbike. So he'd strung the carcasses across the handlebars and down along the pipe thing that goes between the steering column and the seat, and he'd stacked the rabbit skins in a wheat bag and tied it down, tight, on the carry-frame at the back of his bike. Then he slung his shotgun over his shoulder and off into Elliston he pedalled. It was a couple of hours ride or something. This was in the middle of summer and so he was pretty parched by the time he arrived in town and he was even more parched by the time he'd gone around and sold all his skins and his few carcasses. But by now he's got some money in his pocket and so he ends up in the pub.

'What'll yer have?' says the bloke behind the bar.

The old rabbiter says, 'Oh, I'm pretty flush so I might have a glass'a that Grandfather Port, over there.'

So the barman poured the old rabbiter a glass of Grandfather Port, which he downed. Then he downed another one. Then another. And by midnight this old rabbiter's blown all his hard-earned money on Grandfather Port, so he slurs, 'See yer,' to the barman and he staggers outside, slings his shotgun over his shoulder, gets on his pushbike and he heads out of town the long way. By 'the long way' I mean that the bike was zigzagging so badly from one side of the road to the other that, by the time he would've gotten back to his camp he would've almost covered twice the distance.

So there he was, snaking his way down this old dirt track. It's a nice moonlit night, but it's all getting the better of him. He's not seeing too well. In fact, you could liken him to being as blind as a bat, plus he's starting to feeling as crook as a dog. So he decides to lay down beside the dirt track to sleep it off. And it was while he was snoring away he thought he heard a dingo growl and, when he sprung awake, there, just a few feet from his face, were these two bright shining eyes. It's the rogue dingo! he thinks, so he grabs his shotgun and he gives it both barrels, straight between the eyes. 'Boom ... Boom.' There's this hell of a racket, then all's quiet.

'Gotcha,' he said, then he went back to sleep.

It wasn't until mid-morning, with the sun pelting down, that the old rabbiter woke, with a hell of a hangover. The worst he's ever had in his entire life. 'I'll never touch another bloody drop of that bloody Grandfather Port again,' he swears. Then he recalls shooting the rogue dingo. He has a look around. But, no, not a sign. No dead dingo. No blood. Not even a paw print.

'Well, bugger me.' Then it was only when he went to get on his pushbike that he saw that the handlebars had been shot, clean off. So he must've woken up in the night and seen the moonlight reflecting off the handlebars and, in his drunken state, thinking they were the eyes of the rogue dingo, he'd inadvertently blown his own handlebars off.

So that's the story. Now, whether that's true or not, I don't know, but the publican was dead right about one thing: a night on the Grandfather Port gives you one hell of a hangover and so, like the old rabbiter, I swore that I'd never touch a drop of the stuff again.

The Easter Bunny

(More Great Australian Flying Doctor Stories)

In total I worked with the Royal Flying Doctor Service for nine years. That was at both their Broken Hill and Dubbo bases. For much of that time I was employed as an emergency flight nurse and well, in the end, I more or less left because I got married and we moved over here to Walgett, in the central north of New South Wales. That's the only reason why I finished up. But I really loved my time with the RFDS, and I actually kept a diary through the years I was working for them so I've looked up a few stories, if you're interested. I guess they're both about determination of spirit, but in very different ways. What's more, both incidents happened up at Tibooburra, in the far north-western corner of New South Wales.

Well first: one time we got a phone call from a very distressed husband up at Tibooburra. He told us that he'd delivered their last nine babies, all by himself, and there'd been no problems. That's right, nine! And he'd delivered every one of them. But now he said that he was having a bit of trouble delivering their tenth baby. His wife had been in labour for quite a while and, to make matters worse, she didn't want any medical help. In actual fact, she was adamant that there be no medical intervention. No doctors. Nothing. She wanted all home births — just natural — and that was that. No argument. So there he was, this distraught husband, hiding in the next room, out of earshot from his wife, whispering to us over the phone, 'The baby just won't come. What to do?'

From what he was telling us, we surmised it was probably a breech birth because it wasn't coming down well at all. Anyhow, we had a clinic plane in the area so we sent that out and, you know, they arrive and they went in to see how the wife was going and she gets very upset, particularly with her husband, because he'd gone against her wishes and he's asked us to come in to help her. In fact, she's downright angry with him. She was still in labour at that stage and had been for a good twenty-four hours or so, which was very unusual for a tenth child. They should come, probably, within about an hour.

So they tried to settle her down and talk her into coming back down to Broken Hill with them to have the baby in the hospital there. Anyhow, much against her wishes, they eventually managed to coax her on the aircraft and I was in radio contact, waiting at the other end for them in Broken Hill.

There was little change during the flight but then, just as the clinic plane was coming into Broken Hill, they told me over the radio that they thought the baby was coming. So I was telling them what to do and where to find the delivery packs on the aircraft. Still and all, she hadn't had the baby by the time they landed so I got straight onto the aircraft and helped the woman out into the waiting ambulance. Even at that stage she was still complaining about our intervention.

Then, just as we were going over the bridge on our way to the Broken Hill Hospital, we delivered a breech baby in the back of the ambulance. So, we ended up with a hell of a mess and I virtually finished cleaning up the baby and the woman in the ambulance bay of the Broken Hill Hospital.

Now, once the placenta is delivered the mother, more or less, stops bleeding and she can stay fairly comfortable. Anyhow, after I'd cleaned everything up, I turned around to the woman and I said, 'Look, how about we just take you into the hospital and get you checked out?'

But the attitude of the woman hadn't changed one little bit. 'No, no,' she said, 'it's alright.' And she packed the placenta up and she wrapped the baby up and she wandered off to get a taxi downtown so that she could catch the next bus straight back to Tibooburra.

I tell you, it's amazing some of the mums you come across. She was a tough one, alright. And this was her tenth child. But I did feel for her poor husband. I imagine he would've been in the bad books for quite a while, after she got home.

So that was one incident, and the second one was ... well, actually, you do have to laugh at times, don't you? As I said, it's another one about the strength of spirit but in a very different and funny sort of way.

This happened around Easter time and we got a call from the bemused nurses up at Tibooburra saying that they'd just been out in the ambulance and picked up a man who'd been wandering down the Barrier Highway in quite a distressed state. Now, it was extremely hot at the time and, as it turned out, this man was schizophrenic and he'd either broken out, or got out, of a Psychiatric Hospital near Morisset, which is just south of Newcastle, on the central coast of New South Wales. How on earth he found his way out to Tibooburra, I couldn't tell you. I wouldn't have a clue.

Anyhow, he'd told the nurses at Tibooburra that the reason why he was in the area was that he was off to pick pears. Now, mind you, we are talking about the far north-western corner of New South Wales and, as you might imagine, the nearest pear orchard could've been anywhere up to 1000 or so kilometres away. So I think he was in the wrong place.

But, that's not all. What really got the nurses going was that this poor man was not only off to pick pears but he'd also somehow got it in his head that he was the Easter Bunny. So when they found him, he was walking down the road stark naked, apart from wearing his underpants on his head and, for added effect, he'd stuck a carrot up where he shouldn't have — up his rectum. But the nurses said that he wasn't violent or anything because, apparently, when they went out to get him, they simply stopped and asked him if he'd like to hop in the back of the ambulance and in he hopped, no problem at all.

Anyhow, first of all, we found out where this man's father was and contacted him because we thought he might be worried about his missing son. But when we got on to his father and explained the circumstances all he said was, 'Yes, he does that kind of thing, quite a bit. You should've seen what he did last Christmas.'

So then, we flew out to get him and we took him back to Sydney and, again, he got in the plane, no problems at all. But, oh, he was totally off the planet. He had no idea where he was or who he was, other than believing he'd come out to Tibooburra to pick pears and that he was the Easter Bunny. And, what's more, there was no way he was going to let us take his underpants off his head or take the carrot out of his rectum. In his mind, he was the Easter Bunny and that was it. So he stayed that way the whole trip back to Sydney. But you'd think it'd be uncomfortable, wouldn't you, particularly with the carrot.

Classic Westerns

(Great Australian Shearing Stories)

Now old Tolly Bowden was a sort of legend around here, around the Charleville area, in the central southeast of Queensland. He was a top shearer and a top bloke as well, once you got to know him. But there were a couple of things about Tolly that made him different. First, he was one of the most competitive shearers that you're ever likely to find and, second, he couldn't read or write to save his life. Now all this begs a couple of stories or two.

The first one's to do with old Toll's competitive spirit. See, he was so desperate to be the top shearer in the area, the gun as they're called, that he once vowed to take on all comers. Anyhow this announcement happened around the time that the film *The Guns of Navarone* came out this way. So one Saturday night a few of the shearers were getting themselves ready to go into town to see the show. There they were, sprucing themselves up, when in came Tolly.

'Where youse fellers goin'?' he asked.

'Oh,' they said, 'we're off to see *The Guns of Navarone*.'

Now old Toll wasn't that much up with the films and, being the sort of competitive bloke he was, he jumped to the conclusion that his mates were going into town to socialise with some gun shearers who came from some place called Navarone. Now just the thought of it got old Toll all riled up.

'Hey, when you see them guns from Navarone,' he snapped, 'you just tell 'em, if they wanta come out here, I'll give 'em a bloody shearing lesson they'll never forget.'

So that's just how competitive Tolly Bowden was.

Another story, and this one's more to do with him not being able to read or write, was about the time he went to Brisbane with a shearing mate. So there they were in the big smoke and they wanted to get onto this tram. The only trouble was that there was quite a line-up of people all waiting to get onto the same tram.

Now, coming from the bush like he did, old Toll started to panic at the thought of the tram taking off before he had the chance to get on. 'Bugger this,' he said to his mate, and he shoved his way to the front of the queue. As you might imagine, this didn't go down too well with the other people waiting in the line. Nor did it go down well with the tram conductor.

'Hey, feller,' the conductor called out while pointing to a sign, 'can't yer read? That sign says "wait".'

And old Toll, not being able to read, well, he turned to that conductor feller and he said, 'Well mate,' he said, 'I were 9 stone 10 when I left Charleville!'

Then there was the time he was out shearing and he got a mad crush on this housemaid; ended up marrying her, he did. But at that time he was real gone over her, he was. But the problem was, to get to see her, he had to find an excuse to get up to the station homestead where she lived and worked.

Anyway, one day Tolly was having a bit of a natter to the cocky who owned the station and the cocky happened to mention that he had a library full of classic Western paperback books. Now this gave old Toll just the excuse he needed to visit the homestead.

'Oh,' he said to the station owner, 'do yer mind if I come up ta the homestead sometime 'n borra one of them classic Westerns from yer?'

'Not at all,' replied the cocky. 'Not at all.'

So that night, who should arrive on the doorstep of the homestead, all done up to the nines and smelling like roses, none other than old Toll. Of course the cocky wasn't aware that he couldn't read or write and neither did he know that the only reason he'd come up there was to get a closer gawk at the housemaid.

'I just come ta borra one of them classic Westerns yer told me about,' Tolly said.

Anyway, the cocky invited him into the loungeroom where he took one of the paperbacks off the shelf and handed it to the illiterate shearer.

'Thanks,' said old Toll, and then he hung around looking like he wanted to have a chat.

So that's what they did. The two of them sat down and had a chat about this, that and the other. The only trouble was that the cocky soon noticed that Tolly's eyes kept wandering off toward the kitchen where the housemaid was and, when she came into the room, the shearer seemed to lose the complete thread of the conversation and turn into a gibbering idiot.

'Well, yer'd better be off and read that classic Western then, Toll,' said the cocky after he'd run out of things to talk about.

'Oh, okay,' replied old Toll, sounding disappointed. Anyway, off went Tolly, back down to the shearers' quarters with the paperback in his hand.

So that was that. But then the next night, who should turn up on the doorstep of the homestead again, all dressed to kill? None other than old Toll.

'Here, I finished that book, boss,' he said, handing over the paperback. 'So I just come ta grab anotherie.'

So they went inside where the cocky took another classic Western down off the shelf and gave it to Tolly. Then old Toll hung around for a while, making small talk and ogling the housemaid until the owner had run out of things to talk about.

'Well, Toll,' he said, 'yer'd better be off and read that classic Western then.'

'Oh, okay,' replied old Toll, sounding disappointed. Now this went on night after night with Tolly arriving on the doorstep, all done up, saying that he'd read the classic Western he'd been given the previous night and wanting to borrow another one. Then he'd hang around the place, making small talk while he ogled the housemaid.

Any rate, the cocky somehow got wind of the fact that the old shearer couldn't read or write and, what's more, the only reason he came up to the homestead was to eye off this housemaid. So old Toll arrived one night as usual but, instead of being given a classic Western to read, the cocky handed him the telephone directory.

'Well, yer'd better be off and read that classic Western then, Toll,' said the cocky. 'She's a big one tonight.'

'Oh, okay,' replied old Toll, sounding very disappointed.

Anyhow, the next morning they were down at the shearing shed and the cocky said to Tolly, 'Have yer finished that book I gave yer last night, Toll?'

'Yeah,' came the reply.

'And how'd it go?' asked the cocky.

'Oh,' said old Toll, 'it were pretty much like all them other classic Westerns. The good bloke got the woman in the end.'

The Trailer

(Great Australian Outback Police Stories)

Well, I don't think I should give too many of my personal details due to the current police investigations, but my name is Bob and I live in the Sydney suburb of Petersham. As you can see, I'm middle-aged. I pride myself on being family orientated. I have a beautiful wife, Joyce, and two great pre-teenage kids, Samantha and Thomas. I've worked in railway maintenance ever since I left school at sixteen. I started out as an apprentice fitter and turner and I've worked my way up to foreman. So I guess you could say that I'm a very stable sort of bloke. In fact, Joyce often describes me as being 'the rock' in our relationship; most probably due to the fact that I'm the one who tends to remain calm during whatever crises may arise.

As far as the wider family go, my parents passed away quite a few years ago. Then Joyce and I had been caring for her parents up until Joyce's father, Stan, died a couple of years ago. That left Dot — Grandma or Gran, as we all called her — as the only remaining grandparent to the kids. But after Stan's untimely death, Gran's health rapidly went downhill, so much so that, with me still working and Joyce having her part-time job down at the chemist's, it got to the stage where she needed full-time care. That proved to be a very stressful time for us all; firstly of having to go through the process of finding somewhere decent for her to live, then more recently on the day we had to take her to Summer Hill Rest Home.

That was terrible. The poor old girl, we just about had to prise her out of her bedroom on the morning she left. It broke our hearts. That was one of those times when I really had to remain as calm as possible, just to help get us all through the day. Though between you and me, I did shed a tear later on, when nobody was around. Of course, then it took our dear Gran a good while to settle down in the facility. But she's a tough old girl and I think, deep down, she realised how we couldn't manage to look after her any more. So, in the end, things have worked out okay, I guess.

Anyway, enough of that.

Then it would've been in about March when Joyce started to receive emails with regard to her side of the family having a reunion during the September school holidays. It was to be held out the west of New South Wales at Joyce's home town of Wilcannia. Initially I wasn't that keen on going. A few years back we'd gone to one of their so-called family get-togethers and it'd nearly ended up in an all-in brawl. But seeing how Joyce had always been keen for the kids to keep in touch with her side of the family — something I'm fully supportive of — I felt obliged to take them.

At first we were hoping we could get away without Grandma knowing. But after one of the kids, Samantha I think it was, let slip about the reunion, there was no way known that we were going to go out to Wilcannia without her. Actually, I really had my doubts about her going on such a trip. I said, 'But, Gran, don't you think you're a bit too frail to go on such a long trip?'

'I'll be all right. No need to worry about me,' she replied, ever the trooper.

But there was a glimmer of hope in as much as we only had a small two-door Cortina and I'd worked out that, by the time I fitted Joyce and the kids in, plus all the goods and chattels we needed for the two-week trip, there'd be no room for Grandma. So on our next visit I mentioned it to Grandma. I said, 'Look, Gran, I'm afraid there may not be enough room in the car for you.'

That's when she mentioned I should hire the trailer. She'd kind of snookered me there. So the day before we set off I got a tow bar fitted to the Cortina and then I hired a small trailer from a friend of a friend of a friend who charged like a wounded bull.

'Fifty bucks a week plus another five for the tarpaulin, and if you want a spare tyre that'll be another twenty-five bucks.'

With time running short, I agreed. 'Yeah, all right then,' I said and early the following morning Joyce and I packed our goods and chattels into the trailer and the car boot, the kids into the back of the car, and off we went to pick up Grandma from Summer Hill Rest Home.

Of course, by the time we arrived, she'd already packed and had been waiting in the foyer for at least an hour. So into the back of the Cortina she got, in between Samantha and Thomas, and off we went, up Parramatta Road, onto the Great Western Highway, through St Marys and on to Penrith. Then while we were winding our way up the eastern slopes of the Blue Mountains, I just happened to glance in the rear-vision mirror and notice that Gran wasn't looking too well.

'You okay in the back there, Gran?' I called out above the excited noise of the kids.

'Yes, I'm okay,' she said. 'I'll be fine as fine as Larry, just as soon as we get over the mountains.'

Though by the time we'd zig-zagged down the western side of the Great Divide and into Lithgow, it was clear that she wasn't too well at all. Even Joyce had begun to worry. Luckily the kids hadn't noticed that anything was awry and they just continued to niggle each other, as young kids do. Still, when we reached Bathurst I suggested we take a travel break and enjoy a nice picnic lunch. Which everyone agreed to. But after I'd laid down the picnic blanket and Joyce had taken out the Thermos and the curried egg sandwiches she'd prepared earlier that morning, Gran decided to stay in the car. 'I'm all right,' she said, 'No need to worry. Just need to catch my breath.'

It was then that I suggested to Joyce how it may be best if we stay over in a motel at Dubbo that night, just to allow Grandma a bit of extra time to recover from the ordeal of crossing the Blue Mountains.

So we did. Later that afternoon I found a small, reasonably priced hotel on the western outskirts of Dubbo and we settled in; one family room and a single room for Grandma, just so she could get some peace and quiet. Then after a take-away Chinese meal — of which Gran ate very little — she decided to turn in early. The kids turned on the telly, Joyce turned on her laptop and I began to silently wonder if bringing Grandma with us on such a long trip was really the wisest thing to have done. You know, perhaps I should've put my foot down harder.

By morning, Grandma was looking a little better. When I say 'a little better', that's all she was, because she still had a pale-grey look about her and, for some strange reason, her memory wasn't as sharp as it usually was. It was like, overnight, she seemed to have forgotten the names of most of the wider family members. I asked if she wanted me to take her to see a doctor but, no. She'd come on this trip to get back to family and nothing was going to stop her. 'I'll be all right. Don't worry about me.'

'Okay,' I said and I plugged onward to Nyngan. At Nyngan I turned the Cortina onto the Barrier Highway and we headed toward Cobar. Then, you wouldn't believe it, ten kilometres out of Cobar, the back left tyre on the trailer blew — *bang*. And so, while the kids got out and had a run around the bush and Joyce and Grandma sat in the car discussing the possibilities of us all dying out in the vast wilderness of the Barrier Highway, I took the tarpaulin off, unpacked the trailer, got out the spare tyre, loosened the wheel nuts, jacked the trailer up, took the flat tyre off, put the new tyre on and released the jack. When that was all done I repacked the trailer, making sure that I'd tied the tarpaulin back down nice and tight.

'Okay, everyone,' I said. 'Let's head off and we'll grab a bite to eat in Cobar while I sort out a new tyre.'

Which we did.

By the time we'd left Cobar, it was getting well on to mid-afternoon and Grandma was looking quite poorly. Joyce in particular was extremely concerned, though whenever she asked Grandma if she was feeling okay, it was the usual reply of, 'I'm all right. Don't worry about me. Not long to go now, anyway.'

And so we left it at that.

Now I don't know if you've ever driven west on the Barrier Highway late in the afternoon; if you have the option, I'd suggest you don't. The setting sun just glares straight into your eyes, which makes for very uncomfortable driving. Still, as I squinted into the sunset, I took some solace in the fact that at least we were close to our destination, and what's more things had settled down in the car. Joyce's head was now lolling about between sleep and awakeness. The kids had dropped off, as had Grandma, and for the first time on the journey I was able to relax into my own thoughts.

That's until there came an almighty scream from the back of the car. It was Samantha. 'Grandma's dead!' Then, almost simultaneously, Thomas started screaming, 'Grandma's dead!' and when I glanced in the rear-vision mirror there was Grandma, eyes and mouth wide open ... and she was dead.

I immediately pulled the Cortina over onto the verge of the road. I needed time to think. If ever there was a crisis, this was it, and I had to try to remain calm.

Joyce was of no help. She'd shot out of the car along with the kids and they'd joined in a sobbing chorus of, 'Grandma's dead. Poor Grandma. What are we going to do now?'

I then came up with an idea. 'Okay,' I said, 'everyone settle down. We're nearly there. Less than a hundred k's to go, so how about everyone just get back in the car and we'll sort out Grandma when we get into Wilcannia.'

That didn't go down too well. Not at all. No way were the kids going to sit in the back of the car with their dead grandma stuck between them. I looked to Joyce for some sort of support, but she'd turned into a bawling wreck.

That's when I came up with another plan. 'Okay,' I said,

'here's what we'll do then.' And I explained how I was going take all our stuff out of the trailer and then I'd put Grandma in it, cover her over with the tarpaulin and hide the trailer in the bush. When we got to Wilcannia, I'd go straight to the police and sort things out from there.

Nobody had a better idea so that's what I did. I unloaded the trailer and put all our goods and chattels down beside the road. Once that was done, I carefully lifted Grandma out of the back of the Cortina, placed her in the trailer and secured the tarpaulin down nice and tight. I then drove the trailer down a small track, into the bush, uncoupled it, covered it over with some tree branches, just in case, and I left it there and drove the Cortina back out to the road. As a marker to where I'd left the trailer, I made a small mound of rocks on the roadside. After enticing Joyce and the kids back into the car, I stacked in all the gear that had been in the trailer and off we went.

When we arrived at Wilcannia, I dropped off Joyce and the kids at one of the relatives' places and I drove around to the police station. When I explained to the sergeant what had happened, he suggested that, because it was just on dark, it'd be best if we go out at the crack of dawn the following morning and sort out the situation.

Which we did. Just on sunrise the police van arrived outside Joyce's relatives' place. The sergeant had brought along his Aboriginal police aide, 'Just in case,' and so I jumped into my Cortina and the police followed me back out along the Barrier Highway. When we arrived at the small mound of rocks, I led the police along the track, the short way through the bush, to where I'd left the trailer. When we arrived, the tree branches I'd laid over the trailer were still there, but the trailer wasn't.

It'd disappeared. Vanished. I just couldn't believe it. Nor could the police sergeant. Then after the Aboriginal police aide had had a bit of a look around, he said, 'Trailer's been nicked, Sarge. Someone's stole it.'

Characters

(Great Australian Outback Trucking Stories)

A couple of years ago a group of owner-drivers, who'd run the Pacific Highway, asked me to make a speech at a reunion they were having in Grafton. Anyhow, I started off by saying, 'When we began in this industry, none of us made a lot of money ... but Jesus we had a lot of fun.' Then I added, 'Though, unfortunately the fun's gone out of it now.' I said, 'The way I see it is that, in many ways, as the transport industry has evolved, it hasn't necessarily evolved in a good way.'

I said, 'Back in our time the camaraderie was tremendous. If you broke down or you got a flat tyre, a fellow truckie would pull over to give you a hand. But it's not like that now.' I said, 'These days, if you've got a flat tyre, they're more than likely to try and run you over while you're out there changing it.'

And that's just one example of how much things have changed.

And while, yes, a large part of it is probably to do with money, it's my thinking that — and this may sound a bit strange — another thing that's changed the great camaraderie we once had, and for the worse, was when the UHF and CB radios came in. I began to notice it after I got my first CB radio, way back in the early '70s. Like, I've always been a friendly sort of bloke and so, while I'd be driving along, I'd be talking to a fellow truckie on the CB, and we'd chat for hours, nice and friendly. But when I sat down at a roadhouse to have something to eat, and that same feller turned up, he'd go and sit at another table, like I was a total stranger. And I just couldn't understand that.

And another thing, as time's gone we're losing a lot of our really great characters. Because, gee, in the years I was driving, there were some real doozeys. Take my old mate Yappy.

I remember the time I'd dropped off some mining gear out from Townsville, in Queensland, and I was on my way back home to the central coast of New South Wales. Anyhow, I was in this roadhouse having a meal with Yappy. Yappy had just come back from holidays. So this real bushy type meanders into the roadhouse, right? He was your typical outback, you know, with the checked shirt, the moleskins and the RM Williams riding boots. He wore the big Akubra hat, stained and battered with time. He had a real dopey look on his face. His ears lopped over like a Dalmatian's and he talked almost as slow as he walked. When he saw that we were truckies, he strolled over and he said, 'I got a bull out in the trailer. Gotta get it home real quick to Wyong. How long do yer reckon it'll take?'

I forget exactly where we were just now, but Wyong was down the coast a bit, not far out of Newcastle.

Anyhow, Yappy said, 'Geez,' he said, 'I reckon it'll take yer a good six hours ter get to Wyong from here.'

Anyway, this bushy feller leans over real serious like and he asks us in a real quiet tone, 'Fellers,' he says, 'bein' truckies, yer wouldn't happen to have any pills to help me keep awake fer that long, would yer?'

As it happened, Yappy had a bottle of Ford Pills out in his truck. Now, I don't know if you know or not, but Ford Pills are a laxative that's used to relieve bad constipation. They're like dynamite. They'll make you shit through the eye of a needle at ten paces, if you catch my drift.

So old Yappy leans back to this bushy feller. 'Yeah,' he says, real quiet, 'I reckon I might be able ter help yer out there, mate.'

'Oh could yer?' says the bushy. 'That'd be greatly appreciated.'

So old Yappy goes out to his truck and when he comes back he says, 'Look, mate,' he says, 'yer've gotta realise that what we're doing here is highly illegal. So yer've got to promise me that yer won't tell no one that we gave yer these pills, okay?'

'Yer can trust me,' says the bushy feller, with a wink. 'I won't tell a livin' soul.'

So then Yappy slips some of the Ford Pills over to the bushy feller. 'There yer go, mate,' he says. 'There's six there. Take two now and take the other four twenty minutes down the track.'

'Thanks,' the feller says, real slow, and off he goes, on his way to Wyong with the bull in the trailer.

So that was that. Then about six weeks later, old Yappy and me, we're in the same roadhouse, right? And who should turn up? None other than the bushy feller we'd given the Ford Pills to.

'Shit, we're in a bit of strife here,' I said to Yappy.

Anyhow, the bushy feller strolls over. 'G'day, fellers,' he says, in that long, slow drawl of his. 'How yer doin'?'

'Good,' we said. 'How about yerself?'

He said, 'Gee, you fellers must have strong constitutionals.'

'Why's that?' we said.

'Well,' he says, 'them pills yer gave me was mighty powerful.'

'Yeah?'

'Yeah,' he said. 'I took the first two straight away like yer said. Then later on, after I took the other four, I started gettin' stomach cramps real bad.'

'Yeah?' we said, 'So what happened then?'

'Things got worse,' he said. 'A bit further down the road, when I lifted up me foot to put it on the break, I bloody well shit meself good 'n proper.'

'Did yer?' we said.

'Yeah,' he said, 'n when I got home me old man stuck his head in the truck 'n he said, "Gee son, it sure stinks in here. What's happened?"'

'But don't worry,' the bushy feller said, 'I never said nothin' about them stay-awake pills yer gave me. I just told Dad that I'd got a real bad case'a food poisonin.'

Tablelands Highway — NT

(Great Australian Stories: Outback Towns and Pubs)

We live in Traralgon, Victoria, but back a while, my wife, Bronwyn, and I had four months' long service leave owing. So, with our trusty 4-wheel drive and a brand new caravan, we packed up our goods and chattels and our two girls, Madeleine, ten, and Annabelle, twelve, and we set sail on the great Australian outback adventure.

From Traralgon we headed up to Mildura then over to Port Augusta, then up the centre to Darwin, before coming back home down along the east coast. But, when we left Darwin, to head east, we thought, Oh well, instead of going straight down the Stuart Highway to the Threeways then across the Barkly Highway into Queensland, what we'll do is go part-way down the Stuart, to Daly Waters, then head east, out along the Carpentaria Highway, to Cape Crawford, then turn down the Tablelands Highway and drive down to Barkly Roadhouse, where we'd meet up with the Barkly Highway, and then we'd head over into Queensland.

Anyhow, that's what we did and we got to Cape Crawford, then headed south, down the Tablelands Highway. We weren't in any great hurry so each afternoon at about three-thirty we'd start to look out for some side track or other, with the aim of getting settled and having the fire going by five. By dawdling like that it took us two days to go about 200 kilometres, which was okay by me because, in my opinion, camping out's the best part, especially if there's a cold beer available at the end of the day. So then, I'd say, it was at about 9 o'clock on a Sunday morning, we were driving along, when we came across a deserted main roads camp. It was a pretty ramshackle affair with earth-moving equipment and road-making machinery scattered about the place. Then there were the usual caravans, where the workers stayed, with a couple of those transportable loos — toilets — conveniently placed over near the caravans. You know, all the usual for a roadwork's gang.

So that was the layout. Then, just down the road a bit, there was a ROAD CLOSED barricade across the highway and lying up against it was the STOP/SLOW sign. No one was holding it. It was just lying there, semi-propped up against the ROAD CLOSED barricade with the STOP part of the sign facing us. This's a bit odd, we thought; you know, with it being a Sunday and all. Anyhow, we stopped. Like I said, there was no one around so we sat in the car and waited.

Five minutes passed and no one appeared. 'Geez,' I said, 'this's a bit odd.'

'Perhaps they went to Cape Crawford or down to Barkly Roadhouse for a weekend on the booze and they forgot to take the barricade and sign down,' Bronwyn suggested.

She might've had a point there. I mean, these roadworks fellers are pretty well noted for their love of a beer or two or three. Anyhow, we sat for a while longer and still no one turned up. In the end, I got out and checked either side of the road to see if there was any way I could negotiate our vehicle and the caravan around it. But, no, it was impassable on either side. So I got back in the car, and it was while we were sitting there that Madeleine said, 'Perhaps some aliens have taken them.'

I mean, you can't beat kids, can you? Of course, she was only joking, or so I think. But then the longer we sat there, confronted by this ROAD CLOSED barricade, away out in the middle of all this nowhere, in dead silence, with an eerily deserted road maintenance camp just over the way, these type of half-joking scenarios can start to take on some vague sort of reality.

'Maybe,' I said.

Then, 'Dad, did you hear that!' called Annabelle.

'What?'

'It was like someone crying out.'

I tried to laugh that one off, too. But then I heard something. So did the kids. A faint groan coming from over where the workers' caravans were. That got me thinking all sorts of possibilities, and all of them not too good. I mean, you hear some terrible stories, these days, don't you?

'Perhaps you should go over and see if anyone's there,' Bronwyn said.

'Not on your life,' I said. 'I'm not going anywhere near that camp.' In actual fact I'd started thinking that the best thing for us to do was to turn around and go back up to Cape Crawford. It'd only taken us two days to get this far and, if we went over to the east coast the other way, it'd only add another week or so onto our trip and we'd just have to make up some sort of excuse as to why we'd overstayed our long service leave. I mean, as the saying goes: 'It's always better to be safe than sorry'. Anyway, I'd heard along the way that both the petrol and the beer down at Barkly Roadhouse were the most expensive in Australia.

Then came another strange noise from over at the caravans.

'It's creepy; let's get out of here, Dad.'

'Okay,' I said.

Then, just as I was about to start up the car, the door of one of the transportable loos opens. And out came a bloke. He stood there for a moment taking in the scenery. For the life of me, he looked exactly like that cartoon character 'Norm' from those old television ads. Remember the really overweight feller, with the huge belly, who spent all his time sitting in front of the television, drinking beer? And all this bloke had on was an old pair of boxer shorts. I'm not even sure if he was wearing work boots or not; maybe just an old pair of thongs.

And after he'd had a sniff and a scratch, he ambled over to the barricade as if he had all the time in the world and, when he finally arrived, he grabbed part of the ROAD CLOSED barricade and he dragged it sideways. Then he picked up his STOP/ SLOW sign. He had another bit of a scratch. Looked down the road to the south. Looked up the road to the north. Had a bit of yet another scratch. Then, when he'd checked all was clear, he turned his sign around to SLOW and we crawled through the opening, and down the road we headed, with the girls in stitches of laughter and me and Bronwyn shaking our heads: 'Only in Australia'.

West of the Cooper

(The Complete Book of Australian Flying Doctor Stories)

There was an old grazier; for the sake of the story we'll call him Arthur. Well, old Arthur lived out west of the Cooper, around the border area of south-western Queensland and north-eastern South Australia. The name of the station just escapes me for the moment so we'll just stick with 'west of the Cooper'.

Now, what you've got to realise here is that a lot of these old fellers who live out in those remote parts of this wide brown land of ours have probably never been out of the bush. So you can imagine that some of them are probably not quite as academically educated as some of us. In fact, some of them can't even read or write. Mind you, that doesn't make them any less of a person. It's just the way it is.

But old Arthur had a cardiac condition and he needed to go and see a specialist, so I gave him a referral to go and see a specialist in Brisbane. Brisbane was the town of his choice. It wasn't an emergency or anything, it was just routine, so he got on a commercial flight from Windorah and headed off to Brisbane. It was all a new experience for him because, firstly, I don't think he'd ever been on a commercial aeroplane before and, secondly, to my recollection, he'd never been to Brisbane.

When the specialist saw old Arthur, he reckoned that there wasn't much more to be done other than what I'd already recommended he do. That was reassuring to me. But a few weeks later the specialist sent Arthur an account and on the account you've got the Medicare item number which was, we'll say for argument's sake, 'Item number seventy-six'.

Anyway, when old Arthur looked at this account, he couldn't make head nor tail of it. But he did see this number seventy-six. And you know how all the drugs in the RFDS medical chest are labelled by numbers, well, when old Arthur saw this number seventy-six he thought, 'Well, that specialist feller must want me to take number seventy-six out of the RFDS medical kit.'

Then when I was out there, the next month, I saw old Arthur and he said to me, 'Gees,' doctor,' he said, 'that number seventy-six didn't do me a scrap of good.'

'What do you mean?' I said.

'Well,' he said, 'look here: on my account it's got number seventy-six.'

And that's when I discovered that old Arthur had, in actual fact, mixed up the Medicare number with the item number in the RFDS medical kit and had been taking some sort of anti-fungal medication.

The next story also comes from out west of the Cooper.

I got a call one evening — it was after last light — to go out to South Galway Station. One of the ringers there was in some sort of strife. So, you know, we asked them to put out their flares and one thing and another and I told them that we'd be in touch with an ETA (estimated time of arrival) as soon as we got in the air. There was the pilot, a nurse and myself.

Then, when we called through to South Galway Station with the ETA, they told us that there were severe thunderstorms in the area. Now, thunderstorms are a real hazard to flying. First, they can create incredible turbulence. Second, with these being dirt airstrips, they can turn to mud in an instant.

Anyway, the pilot said, 'Oh well, we'll just continue on and see what happens.'

So we continued on. But then just as we arrived over South Galway Station so did the thunderstorm. Oh, it was blowing a beauty and it was raining like crazy. This, in turn, caused most of the flares, which they'd lit for us along the runway, to be either blown out or doused in the rain — one or the other. But fortunately the pilot knew the strip quite well and he reckoned that by using the flashes of lightning as a guide, he could see just enough of the airstrip to land the aeroplane. And that's what he did: he put the plane down on the strip by using the flashes of lightning, along with the few flares that still remained alight. Some of these pilots do amazing things, and that was just one of them.

Anyhow, luckily for us they'd already brought the injured ringer out to the strip, which saved precious time. But even still, with it now raining cats and dogs and the dirt strip rapidly turning greasy, I quickly assessed the situation and decided that if I didn't open the door, put the injured ringer on board, quickly tie him down, shut the door again and get out of there, we'd end up being stuck on the strip — bogged. All patients in stretchers have to be tied down. It's procedure.

So we did that. We loaded this ringer as quickly as we could. Then we tied him down in the stretcher, shut the door, and I told the pilot to get going, which he did, and we took off safely.

But, of course, with this thunderstorm going on all around us, the turbulence was something incredible. As I assessed the patient, we were being tossed around like anything. So I thought, Well, the first thing I need to get into him is an intravenous cannula and a drip.

So I put a tourniquet on him and I literally threw the cannula into his arm like a dart, sort of thing, and it happened to hit a vein. Then I looked over at my nurse, fully expecting her to pass me the drip set, only to find that she had her head stuck in a sick bag. Well, it was all too much for me and I then also had to grab a bag. So there I was, being tossed around in the turbulence, while trying to keep a bag over my face, with one hand holding the drip into the ringer's arm and the other hand trying to put the giving-set into the drip.

And that's when the ringer looked up at us and he said, 'I think I'm probably the best of all of yer.'

Kulgera — NT

(Great Australian Stories: Outback Towns and Pubs)

About twenty k's over the South Australian border, into the Northern Territory, there's this really little place called Kulgera. It's the exact central point of Australia — or that's what they told me at the pub. But, anyway, this happened back sometime in the late '70s. It's all cattle country out there and I was working out on a place for this elderly couple. Real old staunch station people, they were. Strict to the letter. At that stage I was only young, about nineteen, and I'd been working hard for about three months straight, in quite primitive conditions, without seeing a girl or having a beer or anything.

Then come the time for the Kulgera Easter Race Meeting. Now, the Kulgera Easter Race Meeting's the biggest thing that happens in that part of the country and so all the people from off the cattle stations and that, they come in for this big weekend and they stay down at the campground. It's like a big get-together. And the tradition was that when the younger station workers, like me, came into town, we had to hang out with our bosses; you know, set up camp for them, get the fire going, get some water. See, in those days, the boss and his wife were like royalty. With total respect, that's how you were meant to treat them. These days it's a bit more relaxed but, back then, you were expected to be a good ambassador for the station. You know, not play up or nothing.

Anyway, when we got into Kulgera, lots of other station bosses and their families were there and, like, they're all fairly well-to-do and so they're all dressed up and that. So they're all at the campground. Then just up from the campground, by the racetrack area, there was a little hall. That's where all these prim and proper station people were going to have this big function that night. Then just up from the hall was the pub, right. That's where the jackaroos and the jillaroos and the other station workers hung out.

Now, like I said, I'd been three months, living out in pretty rough, isolated conditions so the last thing I wanted to do was to be sitting around with the station bosses and their families, eating sandwiches and talking bullshit. You know, I wanted to get up to the pub and have some fun. So I made up an excuse about how I had to go and make some phone calls.

'Don't be long, young feller,' said the boss, 'you've still got duties to attend to here.' Oh, something I forgot; my boss always had a cigarette hanging out of his mouth — always.

Anyway, I said, 'Okay,' and so I left the campground and I walked past the little hall, then up to the pub. And the place was just rocking and so I started drinking and, well, time just vanished. Next minute, like, it's midnight. I'd been there for hours, you know, just getting on the grog and talking to people more my own age and that. It was just great. Then, about midnight I looked around and there was just the one unattached girl left in the pub. She had a bloke with her but he'd passed out. So she's at a loose end. I'm at a loose end.

Now, I don't know how we hooked up, but we did, right. She might've been, you know, who knows, but her bloke's choked out so she knew she wasn't going to have any fun with him. But we somehow hooked up and I talked her into coming down to the campground for a bit of romance. My swag was back down there. She said, 'Okay,' and so we headed off, past the hall where the posh function was being held. Then, halfway between the hall and the campground, it just got too much. You know, it'd been months and months, and it's a starry night. Very quiet. Dark. I've got a girl who's keen. The crickets are singing in the background.

It was just so romantic and so, right on the side of the road, we started to consummate our relationship. If you can imagine, it was like a scene out of *Gone With the Wind* and *Debbie Does Dallas*, all rolled into one.

Anyhow, so that's what we were doing and, without realising it, the function at the hall had just finished. But I'm so lost in the moment that I didn't even notice all the station people — the old aristocracy — had got into their cars and had started to head back down to the campground. The first I knew about it was when I heard a car horn beeping and I looked up and I saw a woman go by with her hands covering her little kid's eyes. Then, when the next car rolled by, there's my boss, in the passenger's seat, with his eyes popping out of his head and his cigarette falling out of his gob. And just from the look on his face I had a pretty good idea that I'd done me dash. But then, like I said, it'd been quite a while so, after all the cars had gone by, you know, me and this girl, we still had a little bit of lead in our pencils, sort of thing, and we headed down to where my swag was, in the campground. Being dark, no one could see what we were up to and so now it's like Act II of *Gone with the Wind* and *Debbie Does Dallas*.

Then, somewhere along the line, I fell asleep and the girl must've got up and took off because, when I woke up, like, it's broad daylight and I'm just laying there on top of me swag — stark naked — and there's the boss and all his station people, pointing at me and going on. Well, that was it then. I knew I'd get the sack for sure. So I just got up and I got dressed and I rolled me swag and I got out of there and hitched to Alice Springs. Like, you could say, I more or less ran away, really. And that was it for Kulgera.

Dog's Dinner

(The Complete Book of Australian Flying Doctor Stories)

A few years ago there was this feller out on a station who'd somehow got his hand caught in a piece of machinery and had lopped off one of his fingers. Amputated it, like.

So we got the call from this feller; pretty laid back about the accident he was. Like most bushies, real laid back. 'Just lost me finger, doc,' he said. 'What do yer reckon I should do about it?'

'Look,' said the doctor, 'just put a bandage around the stump to stop the bleeding. When that's done get your finger, the missing one, wrap it in a tea towel which is packed with ice and we'll see if we can attach it when we get out there.'

'Ah, doc,' replied the feller, 'me finger's pretty well, yer know, stuffed as far as I can see. It don't look too good at all.'

'Yeah, that may well be the case,' said the doctor. 'But, still and all, grab the finger, put it in a tea towel packed with ice and when we get out there we'll have a good look at it. Right?'

When we landed at the station where the feller lived, way out it was, he sauntered over to the plane. One hand was bandaged up around the stump and he's got a tea towel in his other hand. Both the bandage and the tea towel were soaked through with blood. A real mess, it was.

So we got out of the plane. 'G'day,' we said. 'How yer doing?'

And he said, 'Oh, not real flash.'

Then we asked if we could have a look in the tea towel, just to see how bad the severed finger was.

'Okay,' he said.

As I said, this feller had one hand covered in bandage and he was carrying the tea towel containing the severed finger in the other hand, making things a little awkward for him. Most of the ice had melted, which made it even worse. So when he went to pass over the bloodied tea towel it slipped out of his hand. Before we could catch it ... plop, it came to land on the dusty ground.

Now, that wasn't too bad. But with it being a station there were stacks of working dogs around the place. And all these dogs were kelpie-blue heeler crosses and they all looked the same and they all hung around in packs of about ten or twelve, gathered around the place.

What you've got to realise at this point is that on these stations they keep their working dogs fairly lean. They don't like to overfeed them. That way they've got more stamina when it comes to mustering the sheep or cattle. Now these dogs can smell a free feed from about a kilometre away, and there was a pack of these kelpie-blue heeler crosses hanging around nearby.

Anyway, just as we were about to lean over and pick up the bloodied tea towel containing the mangled finger, one of the dogs shot out from the pack and started ripping into it, tearing it to shreds. We attempted to take the tea towel from the dog but, in a frenzy of hunger, it let us know in no uncertain terms that there was no way it was going to give it up. It was in no mood to have a free feed taken away from it.

In a flash the dog had munched the tea towel to shreds, then it scampered back into the safety of the pack. So we searched for the severed finger among the shredded tea towel but couldn't find it, which left us to assume that the dog had swallowed it. The problem was, with a pack of ten or twelve of these dogs looking exactly the same, we had no hope of working out which one had just eaten this poor guy's finger. Neither did he. He took a look at the tea towel strewn across the ground, then a look at the pack of dogs.

'Beats me which one it was,' he said with a shrug of his shoulders.

'What can we do now?' we were thinking. 'Don't panic. Okay, we can knock these dogs out, open them up one by one. Then, when we find the finger, we can assess the situation and take it from there.'

But the feller must have read our minds. He gave the remnants of the tea towel a bit of a kick with his riding boot and said, 'Ah, fellers, take me word fer it. The finger was pretty much stuffed anyways. What's more, there's no bloody way yer gonna cut open any of my dogs just to look fer me missing finger. I got nine of the buggers left, anyways.'

Split 'Em!

(Great Australian Shearing Stories)

Mate, I've got a story. It's with reference to my dad, who's still alive today. See, us kids were brought up on a sheep station in the west — Western Australia — and, at one time, Dad had this particular dog. A kelpie, it was. It was a real good dog too, a real little worker, like, especially when it came to mustering the sheep up for shearing.

The only problem was that the dog would work the sheep beautifully from the paddock into the holding yard, but as soon as he worked them up near the pen, for some inexplicable reason he'd snap and he'd go straight through the guts of the mob; split them through the middle, like, and make a whole mess of them. There'd be bloody sheep everywhere. So, even though he was a good little worker, like I said, Dad couldn't use him. Useless, he was.

Then one day, one of the blokes who was working on our property, a shedhand or something he was — it might've been Charlie — well, Charlie said to Dad, 'I reckon I can get a lota money fer that dog of yours, if'n yer wanta sell 'im.'

'You're havin' me on,' Dad said. 'There's no chance of selling that mongrel thing. You've seen him work. As soon as he gets the sheep close to the pen he goes crazy and splits 'em right through the guts.'

'Just leave it with me, then,' Charlie said.

So Dad agreed, and this Charlie bloke, well, he went ahead and put a couple of advertisements in the *Country Life* or whatever newspaper was around back in those days. And from these ads he got a couple of inquiries. So one day Charlie came up to the homestead and told Dad that he'd organised for these blokes to come out and have a look at the dog.

Of course Dad didn't believe him. 'Go on,' he said. 'You're havin' a lend of me, I know you are.'

'No, fair dinkum,' Charlie said. 'I'd liketa show these blokes just how good that doga yours is.'

But Dad still wouldn't believe him. 'I tell you right now, Charlie,' he said, 'no one'll buy that dog,' he said, 'and if they do, you can have all the money.'

'Okay,' said Charlie. 'It's a deal.'

Anyway, when the day arrived, Charlie and Dad saddled up the horses and they went out and got a mob of sheep. Then when the prospective buyers arrived they stood and watched the dog work. On Charlie's command the dog took the sheep this way. On Charlie's command he took them that way, always keeping them as tight as a bell. In actual fact, I must say, he did some bloody tremendous work that day and these prospective buyers could see that. They were mightily impressed. Mightily impressed, indeed.

Then Charlie got the dog to bring the sheep into the holding yard, which he did without any trouble. 'Move 'em up,' Charlie called, and the dog started to bring these sheep toward the pen. By that stage Dad was looking pretty tense. He knew the dog and, what's more, he knew that the dog was just about to go right through the guts of them. Then just as he was about to do it, Charlie screamed out, 'Now split 'em!'

Well, those buyer blokes were so astounded at the intelligence of the dog that they almost fought over each other to buy him. Got a lot of money for him, he did, too. Charlie, that is.

Mum

(Swampy)

While Dad was our fearless leader, heading the charge into so many of our life's battles both won and lost, it was left to Mum to fill the gaping holes that remained in our defences.

A devout believer in the spiritual, Mum was born to the notion that all things which moved in the night, or had no immediate explanation, were the working of some mystical phenomenon far greater than the mortal human being could possibly comprehend.

It's not that our family was saved from any suffering because of Mum's spiritual links. No way. We suffered along with everyone else, probably more in many ways.

Let it be understood that poor Dad never had the opportunity to sleep alone with Mum, not for one single night of marriage. Because, always between the nuptial sheets lurked such matter as wrapped-up bricks, bags of corks, rolled-up newspapers, sachets of herbs, packets of copper filings, eucalyptus handkerchiefs, rusty nails and the like.

All these oddities, though not making for a good night's sleep, ensured the morrow to be free from arthritis, headaches, unexplained injuries, bad spirits, and holding nothing but good thoughts, kind deeds, love and luck.

Naturally, none of Mum's strange bedfellows were ever proven to be wholly right, but then again they weren't given the slightest chance to prove themselves wrong. Even when we ventured on our occasional travelling holiday, an extra suitcase had to be lugged along, filled to the brim with this voodoo trinketry, which I came to accept as normal accompaniments to a safe and happy holiday.

Through it all though, Dad held complete faith in Mum. The night before the 1953 Melbourne Cup, back when we were living in Moruya, he slipped the race form guide into Mum's pillowslip. Mum woke the following morning saying she had the strangest of dreams filled with red and white diamonds spinning wildly through the sky. Dad immediately went to the pub and put all his money (plus my piggy bank) on a horse named Wodalla, which carried the colours mentioned in Mum's dream. Dad got 20/1 on the SP. Wodalla won the Cup from Most Regal and My Hero.

Suddenly, thanks to (and unbeknown to) Mum, we were rich, and Dad bought our first car from the bookie he'd just busted. It was an old Holden. But do you think that car would work for Dad. Every time he went somewhere in it, it broke down. That car proved to be such a problem that Dad, thinking the spirits had it in for him, vowed never to place another form guide in Mum's pillowslip.

Though, whenever Mum suggested we take that old car on an outing, it behaved itself perfectly. Many were our afternoons spent amid the various district tips; Dad and me sitting in the car grumbling down our Vegemite sandwiches, while Mum merrily scoured the dump looking for all kinds of odds and sods that'd eventually appear somewhere in our house, if not in my parents' bed.

The term 'Bible bashing' took on new meaning in our household. Not so much for its reading, though God certainly remained high on Mum's spiritual priorities, but more for its treatment of bunions, chilblains, corns, etc. Mum suffered from bunions until she started bashing them with the heavy family Bible, believing the Lord's weight behind the Lord's word could move anything from mountains to bunions.

Many were the times Dad and me would look toward each other in confused wonderment at Mum's goings-on. And more often than not we remained stumped for answers.

But we let it be, safe in the knowledge that somewhere amid this hue of life's strange entanglements, Mum always managed to give us more time than she could afford, more help than we asked for, and more love than we ever deserved.

'X' Marks the Spot

(Great Australian Railway Stories)

You know that song 'I've Been Everywhere'? Well, over my time with the New South Wales Railways, I just about went everywhere. Soon after I joined I was sent up to Tamworth, as a booking officer — booking seats for people, checking things, balancing things and doing a summary of the station's everyday work. Then I went on relief. See, while people went on holidays or whatever, that's when I got shoved out to all different towns. Oh, I floated all up through the north-west to places like Moree, Inverell, Narrabri, Karangi, Tamworth, Werris Creek, Murrurundi and that.

But, in that sort of job, most of your life's spent in the suitcase, travelling from one town to another, staying in pubs. See, when I was away they'd cover for my accommodation and things like that, but when I got back to my home station at Tamworth, they didn't cover for anything. I mean, at one stage, while I was back in Tamworth, I was paying more in hotel accommodation than what I was earning in wages. 'This's not much bloody use,' I thought, so I ended up staying in a private house.

Anyway, after that I went back to Sydney for a while before going down to Junee, again on relief. And, I suppose, I spent about five or six years down there, and I did all that area out the south-west — Griffith, Leeton, Narrandera, Hay, Albury, Wagga and all that.

But Junee was an interesting place. It was a big junction for all the trains, and we certainly had some times. I struck one job there called the Back Shift Roster Clerk. My hours were from eleven o'clock at night through till quarter past eight in the morning, and when you did the roster for the train crews, well, a lot of them had to be transferred onto the trains that were going back to where they'd come from. That's why it was called the 'back shift'. So these blokes, they'd be locals or they were staying in pubs or boarding houses or down the railway barracks. Then, before their train was due to leave, you sent out a call boy on his bicycle to wake them up so they could get ready in time to get down to their allotted train. Now, it was up to each member of the train's crew to let the back shift roster clerk know the time they wanted to be woken up. Like, some of them wanted to be called an hour before their train left, others two hours; whatever they stipulated.

Now, some of those blokes were pretty prickly characters, I can tell you. There was one guard, he was a local — Ken Nuttle was his name, though it mightn't do to mention that. He did shiftwork like I did. I used to stay at the Hotel Junee and I used to drink with him quite a bit. Anyhow, Ken was married and he lived in a house near the pub, in the same street that ran along the railway line. So he lived pretty close by. Ken always wanted to be called exactly one hour before his train departed. But on this particular night, I completely forgot and by the time I remembered and got the call boy to ride down to Ken's place to wake him up, he hardly had any time at all to get himself ready.

So it's two o'clock in the morning and I'm sitting there in the office and the next thing I hear is Ken singing out from his house, 'Parry, you f'n bastard. Yer didn't give me a one hour call. I shouldn't be comin' ta work, yer bloody f'n mongrel.'

Oh, he really went off his beam, you know, giving me this big stir. And on and on he went, getting stuck into me. And at that time of the morning, because the air's so still, all this abuse just echoed around the town. Then, a week later, in the local Junee rag some enterprising reporter wrote, 'All of Junee was woken on such-and-such a night when the back shift roster clerk failed in his duties to wake a particular guard at the appropriate time.'

But anyway, it all worked out okay. That time, Ken only went on a short run — he did his eight hours, like — but when he came back that afternoon I was in the pub and he come over and he said, 'Ah, I'd better buy yer a bloody beer. I guess yer not a bad sort'a bloke.'

So, yes, some of the members of those train crews were very touchy characters. In fact Stan Conroy, a mate of mine, he also rostered the train crews and he had a book and in that book he had the list of their names and beside each he'd either have three X's, two X's, one X or a star, and he'd never tell anyone what it all meant. But he told me. He said, 'Norm,' he said, 'it's me grading system for these crews.' He said, 'The star's fer a bloke who's not a bastard, one X is fer a sort of a bastard, two X's is fer not so bad a bastard and three X's is fer a fair-dinkum downright bastard of a bastard of a bastard's bastard.'

Beaudesert — Qld

(Great Australian Stories: Outback Towns and Pubs)

I've never done anything like this before but I think that some of my stories should be told. That's the way it was in my family. Stories were always passed along. There's one I'm currently following up about my uncle who was a horse dealer and he used to catch a train up to Toowoomba where he'd buy fifty horses or so at the auctions there. And if there wasn't a broken-in horse in amongst them he'd break one in, on the spot, then he'd drive these fifty or so horses all the way back to Beaudesert on his own. *On his own.* So that's just one little story but I need to get a bit more information on that because I've often wondered how the hell he could've managed fifty horses, all by himself.

But this story's just a bit of a yarn about my brother and I. It happened out at a place called Beaudesert, which is in the hinterland, behind the Gold Coast. Beaudesert actually got its name from Beau Desert Station, which was established there back in the 1840s. It's a big farming region — dairy and beef, mainly, these days — set in the valley, near the Logan River. But our family had some property out that way.

Now I'm talking back in the early 1950s, probably about '52 or '53. A long time ago when Beaudesert was a much smaller place than what it is now. Anyhow, the brother and I had been out to one of our family properties, a couple of hours out from Beaudesert, and we were heading home in an old Jeep. We're driving along and we come across this big carpet snake, stretched out across the road. Huge it was, absolutely huge.

'Here's a go,' says my brother and he jumped out and he caught the snake and he stuffed it into a hessian bag, then he threw it into the back of the Jeep and we continued on our way. When we arrived in Beaudesert we had to drive past the Logan-Albert Hotel. We were well known in the establishment so it was natural that we'd call in to have a couple of beers. You know, just to break the journey.

Anyhow, we walked into the pub. To set the scene, it was a Saturday afternoon and the place was absolutely chockers. A real hive of activity. There's SP bookies, the lot. Mind you, it was an illegal operation to run the SP back then. But they were there anyway and they're doing a roaring trade.

Now, with the place being so packed, you virtually had to push and shove your way through the crowd just to get to order a drink. There were two or three barmaids working behind the bar. Not bad lookers either, I might add.

'This's no good,' I said to the brother.

'Hang on a tick,' he says, 'I'll sort this out,' and he disappeared.

Actually, I was hoping he wasn't going to do what I was thinking he was about to do. But, anyway, he did. He appeared back inside with the hessian bag. Now, you really need a cartoonist to draw this but, the instant someone shouted 'Snake!', blokes scattered in all directions. Oh, there were blokes up on top of the bar, blokes up on top of the tables; on top of chairs. Blokes diving out windows. Blokes trying to scramble out the doors. 'Snake!' and blokes just went everywhere. Mind you, some of these fellers were real tough — as tough as nails — you know, men, some as large as brick shithouses. But it didn't matter. They scattered anyway.

'What's going on? What's going on?' the barmaids started calling out from behind the bar.

So my brother picked up the snake. 'Here,' he said, 'this's what's going on,' and he dropped it over their side of the bar.

Well, these barmaids almost shit themselves. They took off into the storeroom and you could've just about heard their screams over on the Gold Coast. The only trouble was that the snake must've been attracted by their high-pitched squeals because it took off after the barmaids. It followed them. Hot on their heels. By the time my brother had jumped over the bar, the snake was already three feet under the door of the storeroom. Anyhow, he managed to drag the thing back just before it completely disappeared in with the barmaids. So then he stuffed it back in the hessian bag, took it outside, and dumped it in the back of the Jeep.

The bar area was pretty clear by then. But we were none too popular. We'd upset the barmaids. The drinkers were peeved about having their Saturday afternoon, down the pub, disturbed. Then there was the bookies. They'd lost a lot of business because, by the time things had returned to normal, the race meeting at Eagle Farm was well and truly over.

So, all in all, things weren't feeling that comfortable. In fact, I'm thinking now, it was just as well that everyone around the place knew that my brother was a Queensland amateur champion boxer or otherwise it could've easily turned nasty. So, yes, we weren't the most popular couple of blokes around Beaudesert there for a while.

Whistle Up

(The Complete Book of Australian Flying Doctor Stories)

A few years ago there were quite a lot of people moving into the pastoral country, out here near Meekatharra, in the central west of Western Australia. Anyway, being new to the area, they weren't familiar with the particular system we had if we wanted to activate an emergency call in at the Royal Flying Doctor base. Mind you, this is well before we had the modern transceivers. Back then, the emergency system was activated by a specially designed whistle. To give you some idea of this whistle, it was about three to four inches long and V-shaped, as in a Winston Churchill victory sign, so that you could blow down each side in turns, one long side, the other shorter.

So say, for example, there was an emergency. What you did was to press the button on the microphone which was attached to the radio then blow one side of the whistle for about ten seconds, then the other side for about six seconds, and that would activate the Flying Doctor emergency call in at Meekatharra.

Of course, it wasn't the perfect system. It definitely had its problems — it was rather difficult to activate the call signal in summer when you were competing against thunderstorms, or if you were one of the older folk or maybe a heavy smoker where you easily ran out of puff. And also, believe it or not, you had to develop a certain technique because when you changed from blowing down the long side to blowing down the short side you only had about a one second gap between blows otherwise it wouldn't work.

Anyway, the bloke who was the base operator in Meekatharra around this time decided that we should set a Sunday morning aside so that everyone could have a practice at blowing their whistles over the radio. Now this was a great idea because it not only gave a chance for the newcomers to get familiar with the system but it also provided the opportunity for those of us who'd lived in the area for a long time to brush up on our whistle-blowing skills.

So on this particular Sunday morning the base operator had us all raring to go. He got us on line then went through the rollcall to make sure that everyone was okay and that they had their special whistles nice and handy, which they did. After that was settled he began to go through the people one by one and listen to them blow their whistles, one long, one short. Quite a few people were successful, others had trouble. That was because they hadn't used the whistles before, or they ran out of wind or, in some cases, the whistles hadn't been used for so long that wasps or whatever had built little mud nests inside which prevented the whistles from working properly.

Anyway, the base operator got to this old feller called Harry. Now Harry had been in the bush for quite a long time and the base operator said, 'Okay, Harry, now blow the long side of your whistle.' So Harry blew into his whistle and the sound it made came over our radios, nice and clear.

'Well done, Harry,' the base operator said, 'now blow the short side.'

Then Harry blew his whistle again and, oddly enough, it gave off the exact same sound. So the base operator asked Harry if he was sure that he'd blown down the other side of the whistle. Well, I can tell you that Harry sounded more than slightly put out by this remark. 'I most certainly did,' he snapped. 'I blew down one side of the whistle, then I blew down the other side of the whistle.'

That seemed clear enough, so the base operator then asked Harry just how long ago it'd been since he'd last used his whistle.

Harry replied by saying that he couldn't really recall the exact date but it was definitely the year when a certain bush footy team took out the grand final.

'Well, okay then,' the base operator said, 'take your whistle and give it a good wash in some soapy water, then shake it dry, and I'll come back to you later and we'll give it another go.'

So off went Harry to wash his whistle and the base operator went on to listen to some other station owners blow their whistles, one long, one short. Then finally he returned to Harry. And when Harry blew his whistle, lo and behold, the shrill came across sounding exactly the same again, both the long side and the short side.

'Look, Harry, there's only the one tone coming through,' the base operator said. 'There must be something stuck down your whistle, maybe some mud, or wasps, or something like that. So how's about you go and get a little bit of wire and have a poke around inside.'

'Okay,' said Harry.

So away went Harry and when he got back on the air about five minutes later he tried his whistle again. There was no change. The result was the same. Still only one tone came through on both the long side and the short side.

The base operator by this stage was getting quite perplexed over the matter so he said to Harry, 'I can't understand what's going on here, Harry. There's definitely only one tone coming through. Are you dead sure that you're using the right whistle?'

'Of course I am,' replied Harry, 'it's the very same whistle I used when I was umpiring that grand final I told you about.'

Gutted

(Great Australian Bush Funeral Stories)

Now, young feller, I know that you've used this one before in *Great Australian Outback Police Stories*, but when I heard that you were writing a book of funeral stories, I said, 'No, no, no, the story is far more suited to that.' So here we go, again.

This is going back before I was born, around the late 1800s, early 1900s — around my grandfather's time — and we're looking up into the central highlands of Tasmania. As it transpires, there's a little town up in that area called Bothwell. It's a beautiful little village, just beautiful. A very frontier type of place with a lot of sandstone buildings. Bothwell was settled by the Scots, going right back. And now here's a point of interest: having been settled by the Scots, Bothwell was known to have had the first golf club in the southern hemisphere. True, so there's a little side story for you.

Anyhow, several miles out from Bothwell was a family by the name of Lawson. I remember the name because I'm a huge fan of Henry Lawson, the great Australian story writer and poet. But this mob of Lawsons lived away out in the real wild country, out on an area known as Misery Plains. And it was a pretty miserable existence. They didn't have any form of transport, not even a horse, so they had to walk everywhere. And they were a huge family. Maybe twenty or more. All inbred, so no one knew who belonged to who. All in together. And unlike the few poor farming souls that also lived out in that area, this Lawson mob didn't own any property or anything. They were more a family who lived off their wits and so they survived by fishing and hunting and there was a lot of poaching going on too I might add, both in and out of season, and it's all highly illegal.

Now I don't know if you've ever had anything to do with snaring or not, but snaring's a very primitive way of catching animals. There's basically two types of snares for land-dwelling animals: 'neckers' and 'treadles'. The Lawsons would've been 'neckers'. That's where you get some rope or wire and tie it like a noose and you attach it to a 'sprunger', which is a supple young sapling. Then you might lay some bait out next to the snare to entice the animal in and when that animal has a go at the bait — *snap* — it gets strung up in the noose and you've got it. Real primitive, like I said.

Anyhow, this Lawson family used to snare a lot of their food; things like small kangaroos or wallabies, wombats and quolls and whatever. But of course, say if you've snared a good number of those larger types of animals all at once, they'd prove to be quite a heavy load to carry home, wouldn't they? Too heavy.

So what the Lawsons used to do was, after they'd snared the animal, they'd rip the guts out of it, right on the spot, which would then lighten their load for the walk back home. So they'd carry these gutted animals home, cook them up and that's what they'd eat; the whole family. It was their tucker, and that might give you an idea as to just how these people lived. Some say that they'd even eat snakes and lizards and frogs, and I wouldn't be at all surprised about that either.

Now, as I heard it, one time back at the turn of the century the policeman from Bothwell was riding his horse through that wild country. Apparently a farmer had reported that some of his stock had gone missing and the copper had come out to investigate. So this copper's riding around the wilderness and he stumbles across the Lawson mob living in this huge old barn sort of thing. As rough as guts it was. If you can imagine a large open dirt-floor space, with a few sheets of holey tin propped up with saplings to make a roof. It had a big old Metters oven up one end and at night they'd all bed down together inside the rusted corrugated iron walls of this barn.

So right out of the blue the policeman arrives at the Lawsons' 'and there's all the family gathered around the old Metters oven, grinning up at him in an odd vacant sort of manner. Anyhow, the copper took old man Lawson aside and he said to him, 'This's just not right.' He said, 'Look at all these people you've got. You just can't live like this. You've got to divide off the bloody house. Turn it into bedrooms and that, to keep everyone separate, you know, from getting into each other's beds and so forth.'

'Yeah, okay,' says old man Lawson.

Then the copper tells old man Lawson that he'll be back in a couple of weeks just to make sure that the job's all done. 'You just can't live like this,' said the copper. 'It's just not human.'

'Yeah, okay,' says old man Lawson, and the copper heads off, leaving all these people huddled around the Metters oven, grinning and going on at each other and so forth.

Anyhow, couple of weeks later the copper comes back to check on the situation; you know, to make sure they'd divided off the barn into separate bedroom spaces. Of course he expects to see all these walls and doors and so forth. But no; what old man Lawson and his tribe had done, they'd gone out and nicked a stack of farm posts, fencing rails and hinged gates and they'd put those up inside the barn. So all they had to do was to jump the fence at night and they'd be back into it.

Anyhow, that was just part of the story because the real one I wanted to tell you was that, while the copper was there, checking on the building project, he was poking around outside and he came across all these little mounds with markers on them. So he asked the old feller Lawson, 'What's the go here?' and old man Lawson tells him that they're the graves of all the stillborn children that various members of the family had had along the way.

The copper said, 'Look, you just can't do that sort of thing. It's illegal. If you don't declare a death you could go to jail.' He said,

'The law states quite clearly that, if there's a birth in the family or if anyone dies, you've got to let the proper authorities know, so that it can be legally recorded. And in that case the proper authority around this area is me. Do you understand what I mean?'

'Yeah, okay,' says old man Lawson.

So that was that.

Anyway, as it transpired, old man Lawson's missus died, so he thinks, Well, I don't want to get into any bloody trouble over this. If I bury her out here the copper's sure to find out and I could end up in jail. So what he does, right, he puts her in an old chaff bag, tosses her over his shoulder and he heads off to Bothwell to declare her death to the policeman. It's a hell of a trip under the best of circumstances, but when it's smack-bang in the middle of summer and it's stinking hot and you've got the dead weight of a quite large woman to lug along over your shoulder, you can just imagine what a walk like that'd be like.

Anyhow, old man Lawson sticks with it and a few days later he eventually makes it to the outskirts of Bothwell. He walks into town. It's another stinking hot day and he gets as far as the Bothwell pub. By crikey, he thinks, I'm pulling in here for a drink before I take the wife to the police station. So he stumbles into the pub with the chaff bag over his shoulder and he dumps it down on the floor.

When it lands with a thud, the publican says with a start, 'My word, it'd be bloody hot out there carrying a load like that, wouldn't it?'

'My oath,' says old man Lawson. 'I'm in desperate need of a beer.'

'So what's in the chaff bag then?' the publican asks as he hands over a beer.

'It's the missus,' he says. 'She carked it and the copper said that, under the law, I had to bring her into town and show her to him.'

'Where did you walk from?' asks the publican.

'Out Misery Plains way.'

'Christ,' says the publican, 'she'd be a fair weight to carry all that distance.'

'My oath,' says old man Lawson. 'She was a pretty hefty woman to start with so, to lighten the load, I stopped along the way and I gutted her.'

Cape Crawford — NT

(Great Australian Stories: Outback Towns and Pubs)

Yeah, Heartbreak Hotel in at Cape Crawford. But first, Cape Crawford's about 300 k out along the Carpentaria Highway, east of Daly Waters. I'm not sure how it got called Cape Crawford other than I think a feller named Crawford found the place. But as to the 'Cape' bit I wouldn't have a clue 'cause it's miles from the nearest sea. But Heartbreak Hotel's pretty much all that's there; just that, the campground, with a few roos — kangaroos — out the back and a little roadhouse part. It's sort of all in one block. Then there's a helicopter space. That's also out the back and they do trips out into the Abner Ranges, where there's all these fantastic rock formations — huge sandstone things like skyscrapers — out at a place called the Lost City. Yeah, that's about it really. So now do you want to hear about the kangaroo?

Well, like, it's real cattle country out there and I was on Macarthur River Station, about twenty or thirty k down the road from Cape Crawford. This's 'round 1999 or 2000 or something like that, and I was working for a contract musterer; a bloke named Ben Tapp. So we'd been, like, working out there for about two or three months without a break really and Ben decided to give us a night off. So probably about four of us, we went into Heartbreak Hotel in this old Toyota with a tray-top back on it.

But Ben had his two kids with him, so we had this governess out in the stock camp with us, teaching his kids every day. So she was out on the stock camp, too. Like, she wasn't that old; probably in her mid to late-twenties. Something like that. And she came along with us, into Cape Crawford. I mean, she was a nice enough girl. A little bit cranky. You know, a little bit moody and all that. Really, I didn't get on with her all that good 'cause, well, she was one of those people who sort of judges you all the time, like, as if you weren't up to scratch or something or not good enough.

Anyhow, there we were, we all arrived at Heartbreak Hotel at about sunset for this piss-up and, you know, if you haven't been drinking for a while it really knocks you. Then, like, there was never any set times as to when they shut the place down. They just shut when they felt like it. So you can imagine what we were like by about two or three in the morning.

Then, I must've just passed out, right, 'cause I got thrown in the back of the Toyota, face down, and the governess, she was in the back too. I just remember Ben's brother, Daniel, was driving and, anyhow, we took off back to the stock camp 'cause we were going back to work that day. The stock camp was around a place called Main Road Bore, and so we're heading out there and I'm just passed out in the back of the Toyota tray-top, face down, and the governess, she was in the back there, too.

And we're going along and I don't know how it happened but Daniel must've hit a kangaroo and, like, he had a few dogs back at the camp so he just threw this dead roo in the back; you know, as a bit of an easy feed for the dogs. So he chucked it in the back and he roared off.

Now, like, I must've been asleep when all that happened 'cause I didn't remember anything about it. So then I woke up, you know, face down and I felt this warm body pressed in against me back, and, like, when you're drunk, you know, you think all sorts of crazy things. Anyhow, I thought it was the governess. You know, I thought, Well, I know we don't get on that good but, like, she must've had a few drinks and she's loosened up and she's feeling a bit toey and romantic so she's decided to cuddle up against me.

I'm still face down at this stage, with me back turned away and so I thought I might try and encourage her a bit, you know, to keep her on the boil. So I reached around to give her a bit of a reassuring touch with my fingers and I felt this warm bit of fur. And, like, I'm still not thinking that straight, right, but the first thing that come into me head was, Gee, she's really come out of her shell. She's even got her strides off. Like, that's what I thought. Then that got me going and so I decided to grab my chance while it was there for the easy taking. So I sort of pulled my strides down a bit. Then I rolled over, to get on top, and there's this dead kangaroo looking at me. So I spun off that pretty quick. But that's when I saw the governess on the other side of the tray-top. She'd been watching the whole thing unfold, you know, and by the look on her face I don't think it helped my credibility too much.

So, yeah, that happened on our way back from Heartbreak Hotel at Cape Crawford.

Cheek to Cheek

(Great Australian Shearing Stories)

Years ago I was working on a property out here in central New South Wales that was owned by the Baldwinsons, Colin and Tom Baldwinson. Anyway I was wool rolling — skirting the fleece. Now there's a slight difference between wool rolling and wool classing. See, when you're wool classing you do one side, then you class. But when you wool roll, you skirt the opposite side from the classer.

Anyhow, there I was wool rolling, and I needed to go to the toilet. So I went across. Now this toilet was unique. I've never seen another one like it. It was a proper long-drop. You know, a pit toilet. And inside there were three seats which just happened to be situated extremely close together, extremely close. There were two high ones and one low one. The low one I guess was for the kids so that they could sit on it. But the thing was, other than the holes being uncomfortably close together, the other thing was that this toilet had only one entry door. It only had one door.

So I get into this thing and I'm sitting down, going seriously, when I hear this motorbike coming along. 'Boom ... ba ... boom ... ba ... boom ... ba.' It was a two-stroke motorbike.

Anyhow, it turned out to be Frosty, this shearer bloke from Blackall. He lives here in Tottenham now. Has for a good while. And Frosty, he pulls up, gets off his bike and he opens the toilet door, and there I am sitting up on the toilet with me pants down around me ankles, see.

'God,' he says, 'why didn't yer tell me yer were in here?'

So I said, 'Come in and sit down and have a yarn.' 'Go to buggery,' he said, and he walked outside.

Of course, I was only joking like. I would've kicked him out, quick smart, if he'd have come in. I mean the holes in there were that close together we'd have been just about sitting cheek to cheek.

So anyway, when I finished I went back over to the shearing shed and I said to old Tom Baldwinson, the owner of the property, ' Those three seats are a bit close. I reckon that they'd cause a bit of a problem every now and then, wouldn't they.'

'Oh,' he said, 'they're alright. The only problem is that you've gotta make sure you wipe the right arse.'

And that's true. That toilet is still there today. A proper long-drop it is, three holes, extremely close together, like I said, and with just the one entry door. So you just open her up and if there's someone else in there you just sit down right next to them, nice and chummy, like.

Bobby and his Mum

(Great Australian Bush Funeral Stories)

I was stationed up in the New England High Country for about three or four years. That was with the police force and we were working out of a place just north of Armidale, called Guyra. Back then it was mostly dairy and potato country, with a bit of cropping and a few sheep. Anyhow, each month or so we'd do a run up through the mountain areas just to see how things were going. Really it was more of a community policing exercise. Along the way we'd visit all the little isolated farms just to say 'G'day' and to see how things were going. One month we might do a circuit out west of Guyra, through Wadsworth, up as far as Tingha, then back around to Bundarra, Abington, Yarrowyck, then on to Armidale and back home along the New England Highway. The next month we might do the easterly circuit out through Wongwibinda, past Cathedral Rock, down to Ebor, Wollomombi, on to Armidale, then back home again.

It was a great day out and you got to meet some of the real 'Mountain People', as the locals called them. And, mind you, some of them were extremely interesting characters, I might add.

One particular family was the Bates. Old feller Bates had died some years beforehand and that'd left old Mrs Bates and her two sons, Eddie and Bobby, to run the dairy farm and grow a few spuds. Eddie would've been in his late thirties and Bobby was more in his early thirties. I never got to see Eddie. Rumour had it, he'd met a young woman when he was in Armidale one time and that was it. They'd formed a relationship and when the woman refused, point blank, to go out and live on the farm with his mum and Bobby, Eddie moved into Armidale where I think he worked in a garage.

So that left Mrs Bates and Bobby to run the farm. It was a tough life by any stretch of the imagination, so it was no small wonder that Eddie's woman refused to live out there. To give you some idea, Bobby and his mum lived in a ramshackle weatherboard house; one of those that sat up on stumps. The roof was rusty. There was no electricity. No refrigeration. No hot running water. The toilet was one of those old drop-style ones, set down the backyard near the woodheap where the spiders and, I presume, the odd Joe Blake — snake — resided. And they lived pretty much hand-to-mouth. They grew a few veggies. They did their cooking on the open fire and they killed a lot of their own food, like kangaroos, lizards, birds and so forth. Oh, and then there were a few trout in the creek that ran through their property, and yabbies of course.

The dairy was more or less a hand-made stone sort of structure, put together many years previous by Old Man Bates, when he first came to the area. Of course, with all the occupational health and safety laws we have these days, they wouldn't be allowed to milk cows within cooee of the place now. But they did back when I was up there. You could still get away with it. By that stage, Bobby and his mum still ran the same number of Jerseys and Guernseys — ten to twenty — that old Mr Bates had run. And, as it was back then, all the cows had to be hand-milked morning and afternoon, seven days a week, fifty-two weeks of the year. So no break.

For some strange reason they didn't have horses, which a lot of the people around the mountain areas did. As for machinery, they had one of those old Ferguson tractors; the ones that were known as Little Grey Fergies. From memory it was an early TE20 — Tractor England — model which had the three-point linkage. They were the ones with the original petrol engine. Great little things they were. Extremely versatile. You could do just about anything with them, which suited the Bates down to the ground. Mind you, in comparison to some of the much larger tractors you have today, like the Cases and the John Deeres and the newer Asian units, the Little Grey Fergies would've looked like a matchbox toy beside them. Anyway, that's all pretty much beside the point though, as you may have guessed, I'm pretty keen on my tractors, the little Fergies in particular. Because, having grown up on a farm myself, I learned to drive a little TE20 Fergie long before I got my car driver's licence.

Anyhow, other than the little Fergie, the Bates had a clapped-out 1951 Holden ute. It might've been the original FX model. It was a real old rust bucket. Bobby and his mum used to drive it into town each month or so to stock up on supplies, and it was only because we were well aware of their dire financial situation and isolation that none of us coppers slapped an unroadworthy sticker on it.

Anyway, Bobby and his mum had lived up there together for God knows how long. It could've been for yonks; just Bobby and his mum. Quite strange they were. In fact, I was always a touch wary of visiting them. Due to their isolated existence they'd had very little outside social contact and so they lacked the usual basic social graces. Like, we were never invited in for a cup of tea or anything. The mum was a real little wizened terrier sort of person who could get quite narky on occasions, while Bobby was ... well ... Bobby was just Bobby.

Now how can I say this in the nicest sort of way? I guess I can't really. There's an old saying that describes someone who's a bit slow or backward as being 'not the full quid'. Well, that was Bobby. I doubt if he'd had much education. With his dad dying when he was a youngster and Eddie having left the farm quite some time back, it'd been left up to him to do most of the manual work around the place. I mean, he wasn't dangerous or threatening in any sort of way. He actually seemed quite a gentle soul. And extremely shy. I never had a real conversation with him. When we'd pop by he'd just hang around in the background and look at us in that vacant sort of way of his while his mum did all the talking. So yes, that's what I remember of him: his vacant look. An odd sort of fellow. But like I said, harmless.

Then one day Mrs Bates died. I'm not sure how the news got through to us at the police station because I doubt if they even had a telephone up there on the farm. But anyway, Mrs Bates died and for some reason, most probably because Bobby was unable to and I was one of the rare people Mrs Bates ever had contact with, I was asked to look after the funeral arrangements and to prepare the eulogy. Which I did. Of course, with them being so poor, it was a simple affair. Just the basic coffin, and that was about it. And because I knew that hardly anyone would attend the funeral, I took along my wife and our eldest daughter, Julia, to boost the numbers. And just as well I did too because, other than Bobby, my wife and I, and Julia and the priest, that was about it. Eddie and his wife didn't even bother to turn up.

So I gave my short eulogy, about how Mrs Bates had lived a tough life and had raised her two boys the best she could under difficult circumstances. And all the while I noted how Bobby sort of hung around in the background of the proceedings, without a hint of emotion. Not a skerrick. He just stood a step or two away from the grave, looking vacantly down on the coffin. In fact, I actually felt quite sorry for him that day. With having lost his mum I wondered how he'd cope, living by himself. Then after the funeral was over he wandered back to his old Holden ute, got in and off he went in a cloud of exhaust smoke. He didn't even stay to thank either me or the priest. That was it. Funeral over, and he was gone.

A couple of days later I got a call from my senior officer: 'Mrs Bates has gone missing.'

I remember my reply being something along the lines of, 'Well, how could she have gone missing when she died last week and we've just buried her?'

'You'd better go down and see the priest.'

Which I did, and when I got there the priest took me over to the gravesite and there was just the big hole where Mrs Bates had been buried, with a pile of dirt around it, and the coffin had gone missing. So I started to have a bit of a look around and that's when I noticed some tyre tracks; tyre tracks that reminded me very much of a Little Grey Fergie. So I put two and two together and I grabbed my offsider and off we went out to the Bates' farm.

By the time we got there it was near on dark so we parked our car a bit back over the rise, out of sight. Then we made our way, as quietly as we could, down the dirt track leading to the old weatherboard house. As we made our way toward the place, I noticed the flickering of candlelight in the small kitchen. So I crept up to the window and took a look inside. And there was Bobby, sitting at one end of the small dining table, eating his dinner and merrily chatting away to his mum, who was propped up in her seat, at the other end of the table.

Denicull Creek — Vic

(Great Australian Stories: Outback Towns and Pubs)

I'm seventy-seven these days and while I've still got my marbles I'd hate some of these stories to be lost. See, my dad was a shearing contractor and I travelled with him to many distant parts of the Riverina and western New South Wales, and so I met some real characters along the way. One in particular was a very well-educated chap called Francis William Carroll. To most he was simply known as Paddy; Paddy Carroll. Unfortunately, he lost his parents when he was a little kid and so he was brought up by his uncle and aunt. Then, in his late teens, he ran away and he came to work for Dad, first as a roustabout, then as a shearer. A good shearer, too. A very clean shearer. You know, like he'd bring them up pink.

Now, other than being a good shearer, Paddy was also a pretty good storyteller. For example, one of the stories he told me was about the first time he ever went to Melbourne. He'd never been to the big smoke before and, for some reason or other, he had to go there to catch a train up north. Mind you, he'd never been on a train before either, so he didn't even know how to go about getting a ticket.

So, anyhow, someone from up bush gave Paddy a ride down to Melbourne and they dropped him off at Spencer Street Railway Station. Of course, the place was pretty crowded, which was something else that Paddy wasn't used to, either. The fewer the people the better was his line of thinking. Anyway, he's looking around, wondering what to do, when he sees a sign saying 'Ticket Office'. That's the place, thinks Paddy, and so he goes over and he joins in the line-up, along with everyone else wanting to buy tickets.

And, well, I guess you know that there's an outer suburb of Melbourne called Lilydale. Lilydale? No, you didn't, well neither did Paddy. So there's Paddy and he's standing in line wondering how you go about buying a ticket. Anyhow, there's this lady in front of him who looks like she knows what she's doing so Paddy thinks, Well I'll just do what she does and I can't go too far wrong. So, when it comes to the woman's turn to buy her ticket, Paddy listens very, very carefully to what she says. First the feller behind the little window of the ticket office says, 'Yes, madam?'

Then the lady replies, 'Lilydale, single, thanks,' and she puts a pound note down on the counter and the feller gives her a ticket.

Good. So now it's Paddy's turn. 'Yes, mate,' says the feller behind the ticket office window.

Paddy puts down a pound and he says to the feller, 'Paddy Carroll, married with four kids, thanks.'

So that's just one of Paddy's stories and, by the way he told it, I never quite knew if it was fair dinkum or not. Like, he'd never smile or grin or anything to give himself away. So he had a pretty laconic sort of manner about him.

Then another story he told me happened at a little place called Denicull Creek. See, back in the old gold-mining days in Victoria, they put a road — a track really — through from Port Fairy, where a lot of the sailing boats used to arrive, right up to Ararat, where a lot of the mining was taking place. That'd be back in the 1850s I'd say. And along this track, each eight to ten mile, there'd always be a pub; you know, a place where a weary traveller could get something to drink, something to eat and have a place to stay, after a long day's walk or ride or whatever. So along this particular road, about five mile south of Ararat, was the small town of Denicull Creek.

To give you some idea, as you come over the Dividing Range

from Ararat, heading south, there's a fairly steep gravel road going down the hill into Denicull Creek. Of course, this story happened long after the goldmining days. By now the area was used more for sheep grazing. But, anyhow, at the bottom of the hill there was this huge bend that swept past the Denicull Creek Hotel and by a huge stand of pine trees.

Anyhow, Paddy was riding his pushbike back from a weekend at Ararat and when he got to the top of the hill he decided to take his feet off the pedals and freewheel for a bit, just to make up some time. But before he realised it, he'd built up such a speed that he couldn't get his feet back on the pedals to slow himself down. And seeing how they didn't have brakes on the handlebars, back in them days, all Paddy could do was to hang on for dear life.

So, down this hill he freewheeled, gathering speed at the rate of knots. And by the time he got to the bottom, and started into this sweeping bend, he was going so fast that he already had the bike lying down on its side. So, to save himself from a complete disaster, he decided he'd have to take the bend a little wider. Which he did by riding the bicycle off the road and up along the verandah of the pub, between the pub wall and the verandah posts. But then, at the end of the verandah, there was a little bit of a ramp where they offloaded the beer kegs, then there was this huge stand of pine trees and Paddy said, 'I remember getting to the end of the verandah, to where the ramp was, but that's the last of it because everything went black.'

Anyhow, he finally regained consciousness on his way to Ararat Hospital, then he stayed there for three days, recovering.

Following that, he spent two days recuperating in an after-care home. And when he went back to collect his bike, he said, 'You wouldn't believe it, there it was, stuck up in the fork of a pine tree, with its wheels still spinning.'

So, old Paddy would've had to have been travelling at a fair clip, ay?

Hot!

(Great Australian Shearing Stories)

I tell you, a shearer earns every cent he gets. Every cent.

Now don't get me wrong, it's a rewarding occupation, but he earns every bloody cent. Just for starters, he has to go out and work in all sorts of strange places, under all sorts of extreme conditions, none worse than the heat. And I tell you, mate, it can get bloody hot out there, stuck in a tin shed, stuck out in the middle of nowhere, in the middle of a heatwave. It can get bloody hot.

Like when I first started shearing. I mean, these days they talk about heatwaves; heatwaves be buggered. These are nothing. Nothing. Now, you mightn't believe this but, without a word of a lie, when I went out on my first run, it didn't drop under 100 degrees until midnight, not for one night I was there. That's true. Every night it'd be twelve o'clock before the temperature fell under the 100-degree mark. That's at midnight, mind you. So you can imagine what it was like during the day. It was unbearable, it was.

Hot, you reckon that was hot. I remember when I was wool classing out toward Brewarrina one time and it was 100 degrees on the board by 9.00am and before smoko it was up to about 112, and it still continued to rise. Up and up it went until it got so hot that the sheep, a few of them anyway, the sheep were coming back up the letting-go pens. And that's no lie. It was a big old shed, on the ground, and after the sheep were shorn and sent outside, the sun was burning their backs so bad that the bastards turned right around and they were walking right back into the shed, just to get out of the sun.

And that's true. Not a word of a lie. These sheep — not all of them mind you, just the odd few — they were standing there in amongst the shearers while they were shearing. I'll never forget it. Congested, but by Christ it was hot. And, as I said to Rooster, as we went across to the huts after our first day, you could not get under the showers. You could not get under the cold water tap in the showers. The cold water would burn you, scald you. And I said to Rooster, didn't I Rooster, I said, 'Look, the silly pricks, they've got two-inch waterpipes just laying out there in the sun, going over to the shearers' huts. And it's like 125 degrees out there.'

Anyway we ran into bloody Matthew Legg, who was only a boy of about four or five at that time, and I said, 'How much water's in that dam over there?'

And he said, 'It's full, Rick.'

'That'll do me,' I said.

So I went across with just my towel and underpants on. There was Johnny Latter, meself, and Stephen Corn — yes, I think it was Stephen Corn — and I just led the charge into this dam. And even the bloody dam water was hot. So I got out into the middle, a long, thin-looking dam it was, and the silt came up to there and the water came up to there and the water on the top was still bloody hot. Still bloody hot. But then, just above the silt, it was a bit cooler. So we bent over like that and whooshed it up over us. Silt and all. It was so bad, mate, that I thought we were going to drop.

God it was hot. You've got no idea.

Talk about hot. I was at one place one time where they had tanks at the shearers' huts, rainwater tanks, like, so that the water came into the huts straight out of the tanks. It wasn't run through pipes or anything. It came straight out of the tanks and into the shower. And even then the water was boiling. That's how hot it was. Boiling. The tank water was boiling. Oh mate, it was a shocker. It was a fortnight heatwave. We even took all our beds out of the huts, all out of the huts, and we spread them out on the claypan. I tell you, I was lying there thinking, 'What the friggin' hell am I doing up here? What the hell am I doing up here?'

Now, while we're talking about hot weather, I'll tell you hot. A mate of mine was at a shed one time and these shearers were shearing away and it was red hot. Red hot. You can't get it much hotter than that — red hot.

Anyway, this shearer went into the catching pen and when he came back out, he said, 'Fuck this. It's too bloody hot for me,' he said to the contractor.

And the contractor said, 'Come on, it's not that hot.'

'Well fucked if I know that, mate,' the shearer said, 'because I just went into the catching pen for a piss and a gush of steam flew out of me!'

Now that's hot.

That is hot. That's bloody hot alright.

Brainless

(The Complete Book of Australian Flying Doctor Stories)

You meet some drongos in this game. You really do. Just take the feller who wanted to go from Adelaide to Cairns. He glanced at the map. 'Ah yes,' he said, 'the shortest way is straight up the Birdsville Track.'

So he set out in the middle of summer in his four-cylinder rust-bucket. He had no spare petrol. No spare water. One baldy spare tyre. No supplies. Nothing. Anyway, he got up towards the north of South Australia and the car broke down.

'Bugger,' he said, and sat there wondering what to do.

Then somewhere he remembered hearing that if you break down in the outback, rule number one is to wait with your car. So he waited ... for the first day, the second day, the third day. By this stage he was getting a bit thirsty. And during the intercourse of these thirsty feelings he looked out over the flat shimmering landscape, and the deeper he looked into the shimmering the more it looked like there was a lake out there, away in the distance.

'There's a stroke of good luck,' he said, and hopped out of his car and set off, walking towards the lake.

The strange thing was, though, the further he walked towards the lake, the further the lake moved away from him. So at the end of the fourth day he concluded that the lake must have been one of those optical illusion things, and he decided that he'd better go back to his car.

He was surely blessed because it was a miracle that he found his vehicle. Still and all, by that stage he was absolutely perishing. It then struck him that the only water he was likely to find in a place like this was the stuff in the radiator. So he tapped the radiator. Now the radiator had anti-freeze in it, and what he didn't know was that anti-freeze contains ethylene glycol. And one of the side effects of drinking ethylene glycol is that it could well cause brain damage.

Anyway, not too much later a car came along and took him into Birdsville where he went straight to the pub and commenced oral rehydration. At that stage the Flying Doctor Service was called and we flew out to Birdsville where we gave him some intravenous rehydration. To give you some idea as to how severely dehydrated this feller was, he was given three litres of fluid intravenously to get just one millilitre of urine out of him.

Later on, in Charleville Hospital, when he asked if there were any side effects caused by drinking radiator water, I explained that unfortunately the radiator had anti-freeze in it and that anti-freeze contains ethylene glycol.

'And what's the problem with that?' he asked.

'The main side effect,' I said, 'is that it could well damage the brain.'

'Gawd,' he said, with a worried look, 'what do yer reckon the chances of me getting brain damage might be?'

I must say that it was a struggle to keep a straight face. I mean, you'd have to be brainless in the first place to attempt to drive across one of the most unforgiving parts of Australia, in the middle of summer, in a vehicle that wasn't in any fit condition to do so, without spare petrol, water or food.

So I said to the chap, 'It's my opinion,' I said, 'that in your particular case, there'd be Buckley's chance of brain damage occurring.'

'Who the hell's Buckley?' he replied.

Jackie

(Great Australian Bush Priests Stories)

Well, I can tell you a bush priest story right off the top of my head if you like. This happened when we lived out on the dairy farm at Monteith, in South Australia. Monteith's on the Murray River, sort of halfway between Murray Bridge and Tailem Bend. Anyhow, one of the things that I have very fond memories of as a kid was our pet magpie, Jackie. I even remember the morning we first got him. My father brought him in and sat him on the end of my bed. He was only a little feller then, just a chick. Apparently he'd fallen out of his nest, so he ended up in bed with me. As I said, we called him Jackie and from that moment on he became more like one of our family. In fact I reckon he even forgot that he was supposed to be a bird.

Mind you, he was clever. Now I don't know if you know or not but magpies are very smart creatures. They learn to adapt, and they learn it very quickly. Jackie's quicker than most, I'd say. Just as an example: see, we had a verandah going around three-quarters of the house and one of Jackie's party tricks was that he could push a tennis ball, with great accuracy, right around that verandah. No joke — and he'd do it at full tilt too. He'd go like the clappers and he'd guide the tennis ball along with his beak.

And oh, he just loved our father. Idolised him, really. Perhaps because it was Dad who'd rescued him. I don't know, but he'd follow Dad everywhere he could. If Dad walked out of the house to head off to work, Jackie would want to go as well. You'd see Dad heading over to the garage and there'd be Jackie trotting along, right at his heels. And Dad would be muttering, 'Piss off, Jackie. Piss off, Jackie.'

Then when Dad went to back the car out of the garage, there'd be Jackie, standing there, right behind the vehicle — sulking — still hoping Dad would weaken and take him out to work with him. But that never happened and Dad would just yell out to him, 'You silly bloody idiot, Jackie. Get out of the fuckin' way or you'll get fuckin' run over.'

Of course, Jackie pretty soon cottoned onto that one too and you'd hear him going around the place calling out, 'Piss off, Jackie,' followed closely by, 'You silly bloody idiot, Jackie. Get out of the fuckin' way or you'll get fuckin' run over.'

Yeah, so Jackie was quite a colourful character. Though there was one thing we had to be careful about: that was when any male who Jackie hadn't been introduced to came to visit. I don't know why it was but he took a great dislike to strange men. Maybe he thought it was his job to protect us while our father was out at work or something. I don't know. I mean, women and children he didn't worry about, but if a strange man came to our house all hell would break loose.

In those days we used to get travelling salesmen and all sorts of people come by. During the Depression era I even remember swaggies coming in to our place and if they somehow managed to get past Jackie, they'd come up to the door and say to our mother, 'Oh, Missus, do you want any wood cut? No money. I'll do it for nothin'. I just want a meal.' Yes, I remember that happening as clear as day; poor buggers.

Also in those days the local ministers and so forth used to go out and around the area visiting their parishioners. Anyhow, this particular day the Methodist minister turned up. Jackie hadn't met him before so, of course, as soon as Jackie sees this stranger get out of the car, he's over by the gate to greet him. And didn't that magpie give the minister a serve. He's swearing and going on. 'Piss off, Jackie. Piss off, Jackie. You silly bloody idiot, Jackie. Get out of the fuckin' way or you'll get fuckin' run over.'

Anyhow the minister managed to make it past Jackie and, when he got to the door, he said to Mum, 'Oh, Mrs Schulz,' he said, 'what a lovely bird you have, but I just can't quite work out what he's saying?'

And as quick as a flash Mum replied, 'Wouldn't have a clue, Minister. He's not even ours. He only arrived this morning. Must belong to the neighbours.'

What's Up, Doc?

(Great Australian Railway Stories)

When I first joined the railways in Tasmania, things still worked pretty much as they'd done for near on the past 100 years. It was still mostly steam, it was the same system, the same type of people, the same operations were still running. You name it, nothing much had changed. So struth, you look back on those days, perhaps not with love but certainly with a kind of fondness.

And mostly they were good times and a lot of hilarious things used to happen, like the old story of stopping and picking mushrooms. I mean, we did that lots of times when we were out on goods trains. If ever you saw a patch of mushrooms out in the paddock, it was, 'Oh, all of a sudden we've got a terrible brake problem.' So the brake'd come on or the brake box'd fall off — any excuse — and you'd go and fill your hat or whatever with the mushrooms. Then you'd fire back on engine and off you'd go again because, invariably, you'd be stopping the night at some country barracks or other and you'd cook up those mushrooms for tea.

But those sorts of things happened all the time. I can remember being told a story. I guess it would've been in the 1940s. Anyway, there was a depot at the end of the Derwent Valley line called Fitzgerald. Fitzgerald's a little scattered town out in the middle of Woop Woop. The main road was only a bush track up on the hill, a couple of miles above the railway station. It's in rainforest country so it's mainly timber industry. But, oh, it was a wild and woolly place.

Now, most of the railway chaps were single men and they lived there in a barracks, which was stuck in the middle of a

'Y'. In Tasmania, a 'Y' is the track where you turn engines. It's called a 'triangle' in other states of Australia. Oh, there's lots of funny things in Tasmania that I can tell you about, like someone calling someone a 'rumone'. That's short for 'rum one'. It's a Tasmanianism you won't hear anywhere else in Australia and it means you're an 'odd bod'.

Anyway, this barracks at Fitzgerald was very small. They only had enough room for four or five single men's bedrooms with a combined kitchen–dining area that had a fuel stove. And of course, being single, all these fellows drank lots and lots and lots of beer, to such an extent that supplies would run out on a frighteningly regular basis. Now, you've got to remember that roads around that neck of the woods were virtually nonexistent, so there were very few cars around. But the nearest pub was at National Park, which is the famous Mount Field National Park, where we ran trains on a regular basis.

So on a Sunday the crews would have one of the locos steaming away in the engine shed, all banked up, ready to run. Then when they run out of grog, they'd all hop aboard and away they'd go. Oh, there'd be about eight or nine of them all squeezed in the cabin, so there'd be a bit of a crowd. Anyhow, they'd tear off down the track, hoping that nothing else was on the line, and they'd head for National Park.

Now, just past National Park, away from the road, there was a cutting and that's where they'd hide the engine. They'd just bank it up, put the handbrake on and off to the pub they'd go. Then after they'd had their fill, just in case of an emergency, they'd buy a barrel of beer, roll it down the track, load it onto the engine, then they'd go at breakneck speed back to Fitzgerald which, as you might imagine, would've been a hairy-scary trip.

But near where they used to park the loco there was a house, and I don't remember the lady's name but she'd see all these goings-on and she'd inform the railway office in Hobart how these fellows were up to no good. But, of course, in those days, the grapevine was extremely efficient so each time some official or other came sneaking around, these fellows would be acting like angels. Anyhow, because they knew this lady was dobbing them in, whenever they saw her standing on the platform, waiting to catch the train, they'd just give her a wave and shoot straight past.

Then there was another train driver called Doc. Doc lived in a camp down behind the barracks that we'd named 'Skid Row', so you can just imagine what it was like. Anyway, Doc kept a cow near the barracks so that whenever the crews wanted milk they'd just go out and milk this cow. Now Doc looked after this old cow like it was a pet, you know, so it was always hanging around the barracks. Then, of course, they had a vegetable garden there, which was another of Doc's pet projects. Having a vegetable garden was very common with railway blokes. They had gardens all over the place. It's known Australia-wide that railwaymen were good gardeners. Anyway, these blokes were on the booze one night, as per usual, and, at one stage, one of the train drivers, old Rastus, he staggered back into the common room and yelled, 'Somethin's out there's eatin' the f'n lettuces.'

And old Doc, who was in his usual drunken state, replied, 'Don't worry, Rastus. I'll sort it out.'

So Doc grabbed his shotgun and he stumbled outside. Next thing they hear is this almighty *Boom!* And you can just imagine it: Doc, coming back into the barracks and standing at the door, with his big hat stuck back on his head, the barrel of his shotgun still smoking. Then he looked around the room for a bit, wide-mouthed, with a bewildered look in his eye.

'What's up, Doc?' the fellers asked.

'I'll be stuffed,' Doc slurred. 'I think I just shot me own bloody cow.'